The CARTONNAGE KIT

The
CARTONNAGE KIT

How to make fabric-covered boxes,
trays, folders and files

HEATHER LUKE

Little, Brown and Company
Boston • New York • Toronto • London

A LITTLE, BROWN BOOK

First published in Great Britain in 1995
by Little, Brown and Company (UK)

Created, edited and produced by
Rosemary Wilkinson Publishing
4 Lonsdale Square
London N1 1EN

A CIP catalogue record for this book is available from the British Library.

ISBN 0-316-91390-1
(10 9 8 7 6 5 4 3 2 1)

Design: Pentrix
Artwork: Stephen Dew
Photography: Shona Wood
Project make-up: Carol Hicks

Produced by Mandarin Offset
Printed and bound in Hong Kong

Little, Brown and Company (UK)
Brettenham House
Lancaster Place
London WC2E 7EN

MEASUREMENTS

Please note that metric and imperial measurements are not exact equivalents: so for each project work in only one system. Different conversions may also be given in different projects depending on the context. Measurements for materials have been rounded up but for card cutting instructions are exact.

CONTENTS

Cartonnage or box making is a traditional craft, most popular in northern Europe during the latter part of the last century when home craft skills were arguably at their highest. Materials of all kinds were made more readily available with the advent of the Industrial Revolution and leisure time among the wealthier ladies was considered to be well spent in the improvement of their craft skills and the making of decorative objects for the home and as presents. Not only boxes but many other practical household items were made from card and covered with fabric.

Many of these home crafts have been revived as we also seek to fill our (much decreased) leisure time with creative activity: patchwork, needlepoint and cross stitch, latterly découpage and most recently cartonnage, to name but a few.

It is still possible to find antique fabric-covered boxes in bric-à-brac shops and market stalls, especially in northern France. They were usually made with a traditional regional stripe or a pretty floral print and the fabric was not glued to the card but stitched in place by hand with such tiny stitches as to be almost invisible.

The first piece of cartonnage that I saw, and which awakened my interest in the subject, was at a village embroidery exhibition which I stumbled upon en route elsewhere. A local collector had brought some beautifully hand-stitched Victorian costumes and with the petticoats and bonnets there was a tiny tray with separate, sloping sides tied at each corner with ribbons, which we presumed would have been used on a dressing table. I have adapted this, my first find and also the oldest piece I have seen to date, to give the dressing table tray on page 54.

Cartonnage did not really go out of fashion in France and Holland but had been considered a child's hobby until very recently when the immense possibilities have begun to be realised. The vastly increased range of fabrics available today and the greater interest in the decoration of the home have opened up the possibilities for the craft. Cartonnage is an especially attractive hobby for those who love to make things but dislike sewing.

Three years ago I met Carol who had recently returned from a short spell living in France where she had attended several courses to learn more about the craft of cartonnage as it is practised today. As an interior decorator, I immediately saw the potential that cartonnage offered for making useful but decorative items - a pile of boxes in the bathroom, pretty trays for the dressing table and side tables, photograph frames, folders for papers, small desk boxes to replace commercial packaging for paper clips and other essential stationery items: all made with card and covered with fabrics to match my room schemes. So together we set about making kits and we now have a full range.

The projects have cutting plans for card and fabrics where relevant and there are nine full size templates inside the back of the book for you to use to make the dressing table tray, the scallop-topped box, the storage bin, the cufflink tray, desk tray and bathroom tray, the single photograph frame, the kitchen tray and the hat box. Trace each of the designs onto good quality tracing paper before you start, so that you have each template for future reference.

For those who love to make but have neither the time nor the inclination to perfect their own designs we have given details on page 128 of where you may purchase complete kits, materials and tools needed, by mail order.

The modern method of cartonnage is to glue the fabric to the card and we have shown this method throughout. Of course, if you are a dedicated needleworker, you may prefer to keep the craft pure and to stitch each piece together, so please adapt our methods to suit handsewing.

There are so many items which can be made from card and fabric that the possibilities are seemingly limitless with ever more unique combinations of fabrics, linings and trimmings. Boxes, trays and photograph frames particularly make lovely presents as one can never have too many in the home.

In encouraging you to experiment and to have a go with brushes, card, glue and, of course, fabric, I also have to warn you that cartonnage will almost certainly become addictive and your new skill will be much in demand - perhaps, after all, it would be best not to show the results to your friends...

The
BASICS

Our instructions in this first chapter show you how to make the basic box, lids, divisions, folder corners and spines, all in the traditional manner, so that the keen amateur will be able to develop and adapt our project ideas to make any fabric-covered card item from scratch. There are some gift ideas at the end of the chapter to get you started. While endorsing the creative possibilities of the craft, I should advise you at the same time to expect to make mistakes as the measurements can be complex and must be absolutely accurate. We still have to practise and often make several prototypes before we are completely happy with any product.

Equipment

1 Craft knife

Choose a knife that is heavy duty and takes replaceable blades, as it is essential for accurate cutting that the blade is always sharp. Keep one blade for cutting thinner materials, such as the thin card and paper-backed fabric, and another for the stiff card. Try to discipline yourself always to use the craft knife and never scissors for cutting card. Your results will be much more accurate. Be careful to cut away from your body and keep your fingers well clear of the blades.

2 Steel ruler

It is essential that your ruler is metal so that you can cut against it with the craft knife. Stainless steel is preferable. Ideally the ruler should have measurements marked on both edges and on both sides. A ruler of 50 cm (18 in) long will be adequate. If working in inches, a ruler with divisions of twelfths and sixteenths of an inch is needed.

3 Cutting board

Self-healing cutting mats are now widely

TOOLS

1 Craft knife
2 Steel ruler
3 Cutting board
4 Set square
5 Scissors
6 Pencils
7 Glue
8 Brushes
9 Point turner
10 Eyelet maker
11 Odds and ends

available and it is recommended that you get the largest size available. They are used for the cutting of stiff and thin card and paper-backed fabric, as well as providing a firm, flat base during the construction of the projects. If you do not have such a board, a large sheet of card (minimum 2 mm/$\frac{1}{12}$ in thick and changed frequently) will suffice, but your cutting blade will become blunt more quickly.

4 Set square
This is used to check that corner angles are 90° before cutting. One made from steel is doubly useful as you can then cut against it.

5 Scissors
Two pairs of scissors are recommended. One should be a pair of fabric shears, the other a smaller pair with, say, 6 cm (2½ in) long, pointed blades and, as these are used for detailed corner work, they should be very sharp. Do not use them for trimming card or paper, as this will quickly blunt them.

6 Pencils
Use either a very well-sharpened pencil or, preferably, the type with an extendable and retractable lead. It is imperative when you are measuring card that the lead is very sharp, as a thick pencil line can throw your measurements out by as much as 1-2 mm ($\frac{1}{12}$ in) at the outset.

7 Glue
Choosing the correct glue is most important. It must be a fast-acting, strong adhesive that is clear drying and suitable for both card and fabric. It should also dry quickly. Throughout the book we have used a white, vinyl-based, wood glue, which should be available from larger craft stores or can be obtained by mail order (see page 128).

Always apply the glue to the more substantial of the two pieces that you are joining – usually the card. Cover the piece evenly and thinly; be economical as excess glue may seep through the fabric and mark your work. Use up and down strokes, then work backwards and forwards at 90° to ensure that every part is covered.

Always lay the glued surface down onto the reverse of the fabric, press, then turn over and, with the palm of your hand, smooth the fabric against the board to exclude all air bubbles.

8 Brushes
As the brushes are to be used with glue, it is a waste of money to buy expensive ones. Rather choose cheaper ones and change them regularly. For all projects in this book two sizes of brush have been used: a 1 cm (³⁄₈ in) for pasting edges and a 2 cm (¾ in) for large flat surfaces – both with short, stiff bristles.

9 Point turner
This is an invaluable tool for cartonnage. It is 12 to 18 cm (5 to 7 in) in length, rounded at one end and tapering to a blunt point at the other. It may be made of plastic but the most durable are made of bone. The rounded end can be used to hold stiff card steady while you glue it and the pointed end is used essentially for corner work but is also extremely useful for neatening edges and for scoring.

10 Eyelet maker
Eyelet makers and eyelets are available in kit form from haberdashers and stationery stores. Eyelet holes protect card against wear when ribbons are used as closures.

11 Odds and ends
Cotton rags: these are invaluable for wiping away excess glue on work or from your fingers (a damp cloth helps in the latter case).

Magazines: always set aside an area that will be used for glueing and nothing else. A useful tip is to use an old magazine. After each stage of glueing, turn the page over so that the next item to be glued is placed on a fresh, clean page. In this way, no odd smears of glue can be transferred to subsequent pieces of work.

Jam jar: try to develop the habit of placing glue brushes when not in use upside down in an empty jam jar. By doing this you will know where they are and will not run the risk of putting a piece of work down on top of one.

Sandpaper block: this is useful for levelling uneven corners, making minor adjustments to the size of a piece of card or neatening card cut freehand. For more intricate work, an emery board is very useful.

Card, cutting and paper

Stiff card

The most versatile card to use is Dutch grey-board of 2 mm ($\frac{1}{12}$ in) thickness. This is obtainable from art and craft suppliers and is sold in large sheets, which can be cut down for the various projects. It has been used for the majority of items in this book.

Also available is a 2 mm ($\frac{1}{12}$ in) thick, white-faced card, which is especially useful if you are working with light coloured fabrics, since it will not dull the background colour.

For most of the projects in this book, one thickness of 2 mm ($\frac{1}{12}$ in) card has been used but where added strength is needed, as in the portfolio on page 118, then either a thicker card can be used or two pieces of card can be glued together.

To measure and cut stiff card

Place the card on a cutting board and choose one corner to work from. With a set square, check that this corner is 90° and straighten the two outside edges if necessary. Measure up from one side and mark the required length with a sharp pencil. Repeat further along the width of the card. No more than two accurately measured points are necessary to draw a straight line. Join the marks and repeat the procedure for the width measurements.

Align the steel ruler on one of the pencil lines and apply firm pressure, keeping your fingers away from the edge of the ruler. Using your craft knife, lightly score along the length of the line, running the blade against the ruler

(1). Repeat using more pressure on the knife until the board is cut through.

Freehand cutting, e.g. curves, scallops

Draw the required shape in pencil on the card, then, making sure you have a very sharp blade in your craft knife, lightly score along the pencil line, trying to keep the motion fluid and steady. Do not try to make too deep a cut at first. By scoring the board you are creating a groove for the subsequent cuts to follow. Carry on scoring until the card is cut through. If the result is a little uneven, use a fine sand-paper block or an emery board to smooth and neaten the edges.

Scoring

Some projects will call for the card to be just scored. This means making a light cut along the pencilled line and into the card but not all the way through it (2). This allows the card to be bent into shape. Always bend the card with the scored side on the outside.

Thin card

Whereas the stiff card makes the basic shape of your work, a thinner card is used to ensure a professional finish to the lining. A white or light coloured card of approximately 250 gsm is ideal, and this is available from stationers and art shops.

Measure and mark in the same way as for the stiff card and always use a craft knife and steel ruler to cut it out.

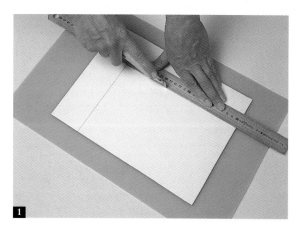

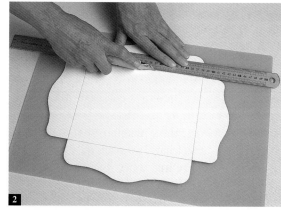

Offcuts

Cutting plans are given for the projects assuming that you are starting with a large piece of card. However, as you make more and more projects, there will inevitably be off-cuts. Save these and use them in subsequent projects – just work from the measurements given for each of the pieces required.

Cutting plans

Cutting plans give layouts for the various pieces. The actual dimensions of the pieces are given in the materials list, with the depth measurement first, followed by the width.

Kraft paper

This paper is used in the construction of boxes to join and secure pieces of card to each other and to reinforce a glued joint. It is available from stationery stores in strips, already gummed or plain, or in rolls which can be cut to the desired width. My personal preference is for the latter as I have found that some pre-gummed strips are made from a thicker paper which shows through the outer fabric more readily. The usual colour of the paper is brown but it can also be obtained in white, which is essential if you are working with white card and a light-coloured outer fabric.

Kraft paper is cut to the desired width (usually 3 cm / 1¼ in) and length, the card is glued, then the kraft paper strips are applied. Never paste glue directly onto the kraft paper, as this causes it to distort and tear.

With pre-gummed strips, just moisten the glue with a brush dipped in water and place in position. Detailed instructions for using kraft paper are given on page 17.

Paper-backed fabric

This is a woven fabric backed with paper which both makes glueing easier and will not let glue seep through to the front. Care has to be taken as glue inadvertently brushed on the front of the fabric will stain if not promptly removed. It has a much greater strength than ordinary fabrics and when cut, the raw edge does not fray. It is only available in solid colours and, although it is quite a dense weave, the raw fabric edges that it is covering will show through. If this is unobtainable, you might use bookbinder's linen instead.

Fabric

The choice of fabric covering for your cartonnage is, of course, a personal decision and many factors will affect your choice - where the finished article is to go, whom it is for and to what use it will be put. However, a few basic points should be taken into account.

1 Wherever possible use natural fabrics, a 100% cotton is especially recommended: glueing is much easier and a better finish is obtained.

2 Be wary of loose weave or very fine fabrics. The former tends to fray and both can distort easily and let glue through. A firmly woven cotton is ideal.

3 Choose a pattern that is appropriate for the item that you are making. A very small print will become insignificant on a large item. An allover pattern will not match at any one point , but do try to use an important part of the design as effectively as possible on the lid.

Stripes will only match on one side and checks probably not at all, so it is better not to try to match than to try and just miss.

Also be wary of patterns which have an obvious direction - pattern direction and matching in relation to the pieces must be carefully thought out before cutting.

4 Do not try to use thick fabric as it will be impossible to produce neatly finished corners on boxes or folders.

5 Fabrics with pale backgrounds and plain coloured fabrics are more difficult to work with. For beginners a good fabric to start with would be one with a medium dark background and a random design. As you become more practised, then you will be able to use a wider range of fabrics with confidence.

6 Many fabrics are printed slightly off the grain. Cut and work to the pattern, not the grain.

7 Before using any fabric, iron it to remove all creases, and when measuring and marking, do so with pencil on the reverse of the fabric.

Cutting fabric

Before cutting the fabric, check the pattern carefully to make sure that you are making the best use of whole motifs and prints which have an obvious top and bottom. You might like to place your cut pieces of card onto the fabric and mark them with tailor's chalk first, so that you can be sure to align any pattern with the card. Leave turning allowances all round, then cut.

Weights and drying time

For many of the projects in the book, it is essential to place your work under some form of weight. Two pieces of card will not glue together satisfactorily unless some weight is applied and, if allowed to dry naturally, a glued fabric will shrink and may cause the card to bow. I usually keep a pile of large books for this purpose. Ideally, the bottom book or weight should be at least the same size as the piece of work, then other books or kitchen weights can be placed on top.

For work in progress, leave the card under weights while you carry on with a separate part of the project, but for the finished work, it is advisable to leave it weighted overnight. This ensures that the glue makes a good, strong bond and the piece stays absolutely flat.

Once you feel confident working with the glue and the cartonnage methods, you can have fun experimenting with fabrics. Mix checks and stripes or floral patterns and checks; put plains and patterns together. Small scale patterns look best on smaller items, such as these little trays.

A basic box

The following detailed method is the basis for making any size of square or rectangular box and should be referred to when making any such project from this book. I have also given the formula for making boxes to any dimension, so that you can make a box to the size of your choice.

Adjacent and upper sides

A box is constructed from five pieces of stiff card: a base to which four sides are attached with kraft paper and glue. The sides are worked in pairs, known as the adjacent sides and the upper sides, and these names are indicative of the roles that they play in the construction of a box.

Adjacent sides are those that abut or lie next to the base and they are opposite each other. These two sides are glued into position first.

Upper sides are glued in place next and are positioned on top of the base, between the adjacent sides.

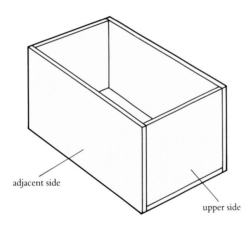

adjacent side

upper side

Krafting

The technique for fixing the sides in place is known as krafting. Strips of kraft paper are cut to the length of the card you are working on, then glued in place. A 3 cm (1¼) width should be used unless otherwise specified. The golden rule here is always apply glue to the card and never to the kraft paper.
As mentioned above, glue is always applied to the more substantial of any two pieces.

Card dimensions

For all the projects in this book, exact dimensions are given for the card that is needed, but you may well wish to make boxes to your own specific size. The following formula will give you the amount of card needed.

For a box using 2 mm (¹⁄₁₂ in) thick card

1 Measure or calculate the outside height of the box. Call it A.
2 Adjacent side (usually the longer side of a rectangular box or the front of a box with a hinged lid):
Measure or calculate the outside length and call this B.
3 Upper side:
Measure or calculate the outside width and subtract 4 mm (⅙ in). Call this C.

Substitute your measurements in the following formula and cut the number of pieces specified:
adjacent sides: A x B – cut two
upper sides: C x (A minus 2 mm / ¹⁄₁₂ in) – cut two
base: B x C – cut one

For a separate box lid

Make up the box.
1 Decide on the required depth of the lid and call this A.
2 Adjacent side:
Measure the overall length of the box and add 7 mm (⁵⁄₁₆ in). Call this B.
3 Upper side:
Measure the overall width of the box and add 3 mm (⅛ in). Call this C.

Substitute your measurements in the following formula and cut the number of pieces specified:
adjacent sides: A x B – cut two
upper sides: C x (A minus 2 mm/¹⁄₁₂ in) – cut two
base: B x C – cut one

The following instructions are for a basic box to which you can add a hinged or a separate lid as described on pages 18 to 23.

Making a box

This basic method is used in the construction of boxes of all shapes and sizes. The pencil pot, wine box, book box and card box at the end of the chapter (pages 31 to 37) show just a few of the many practical applications of the technique.

1 First cut the card following the guidelines on page 12. Take a strip of kraft paper 3 cm (1¼ in) wide and fold in half lengthways, matt side to the middle. Cut four strips equal in length to the four sides of the base of the box. Paste a 1.5 cm (⅝ in) strip of glue to one side of the base, using a 1 cm (⅜ in) wide brush, open out the corresponding kraft strip and slip it onto the base so that one half is glued and the other half forms a free flap. Repeat for the other three sides (1).

You will now have a base with four free flaps to which you can apply the sides.

2 Start with the adjacent sides. Paste a strip of glue to the bottom of one side and line this up against the base piece, glued side out. With the help of a point turner, press the base flap up against the glued side until you have a smooth and firm adhesion. Wipe away excess glue with a cotton rag and hold for a few seconds while the glue dries.

Construct the other adjacent side in exactly the same way (2).

3 Take an upper side and paste glue in a strip along the bottom as for the previous sides and also on three of the thin edges of the card - the bottom and the two sides. Slide this upper side into position between the two adjacent sides and sit it on top of the base (3). Press the base flap up as before.

Cut two pieces of folded kraft paper to the height of the box. Paste glue to the outside corner angle of the box, then slide the kraft paper into position and press carefully. Cover the other outside corner angle with kraft paper in the same way.

4 Turn the box flat on this upper side on a firm surface and, with the point turner, press against all three inside angles. This ensures that the upper side is positioned as flat and as accurately as possible.

With further strips of kraft paper, cover all the inside angles to reinforce the structure of the box.

Repeat this procedure for the other upper side. Finally check that all corners and angles both inside and out have been covered with kraft paper.

Leave the box to dry. Once dry, check that the corners on the top of the box are level. If they are not, use a fine sandpaper block to level them.

Attached lid, hinged & padded

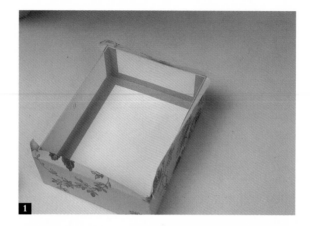

1 First cover the outside of the box. Mark the letter H on one of the adjacent sides to indicate that this will be the hinged side. Measure the internal dimensions of the box and make a note of these for later.

From the fabric that you have chosen to cover the box, measure and cut a piece that is the length of:
- the upper side x 2 + adjacent side + 2 cm (¾ in)
and the width of:
- the height of the box + 3 cm (1¼ in)

Ensuring that there is a 1.5 cm (⅝ in) over–lap at top and bottom, glue the fabric onto the box by wrapping it round the sides in the following order:

place 1 cm (⅜ in) onto the designated H side, then cover the adjoining upper side, front adjacent side, next upper side and finally 1 cm (⅜ in) onto the opposite edge of the H side **(1)**.

2 At the bottom of the box, pinch the 1.5 cm (⅝ in) overlap of fabric flat against the base of the box **(2)**, cut off the excess and glue the resulting flaps down.

3 At the top of the box, cut away the excess fabric at each corner **(3a, b and c)** and glue the flaps down.

4

5

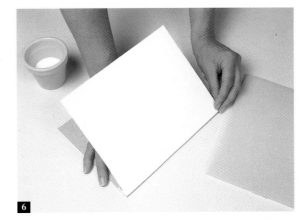

6

7

4 To make the internal hinge, cut a strip of lining material that is the exact width of the inside of the hinge side times the height of the box plus 5 cm (2 in). Paste glue to the inside of the H side plus a 1 cm (⅜ in) band on the base of the box and press the lining in place. The resulting top flap of approximately 4 cm (1¼ in) should be left free at this stage.

5 To line the box, choose one of the methods described on page 24. If lining with paper-backed fabric, you will only have three sides to cover, as the fourth side has already been covered by the hinge fabric (**4 and 5**). If using lining cards, you will need four pieces for the four sides.

6 For the hinged lid the dimensions of stiff card required are:
- the width of the box (i.e. side to side) + 4 mm (⅙ in) x the depth of the box (i.e. front to back) + 2 mm (1/12 in).
Mark an H on one of the width sides to correspond to the side of the box marked H. Using the stiff card as a template, cut a piece of thin card that is exactly the same width but 2 cm (¾ in) longer. Place the stiff card on top of the thin card and score lightly along the 2 cm (¾ in) overlap. Fold back and glue this strip along the edge of the lid marked H. This makes a pocket in which the wadding will be placed (**6**).
Cut a piece of wadding that is 5 mm (¾ in) smaller all round than the lid. Set aside.

7 Take a piece of outer fabric that is at least 4 cm (1½ in) wider than the box lid and longer than the lid by the depth of the box + 4 cm (1½ in). Paste glue to the thin card and press onto the fabric, so that the hinge of the pocket is positioned towards the centre and there is a 2 cm (¾ in) fabric overlap on the other three (open) sides (**7**). Turn over,

8

9

smooth out any air bubbles, then turn back and mark the fabric as shown in the diagram below. Cut along the dotted lines to remove the shaded areas, taking care not to cut off the tabs.

width of the fabric hinge should be exactly the same as the box, but if it is slightly too wide, then trim carefully to size. Glue the remaining flap onto the base of the box. Do not now open the box until it has fully dried or the hinge will be weakened.

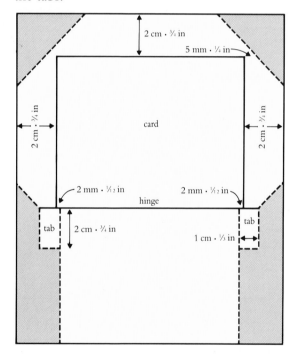

2 cm · ¾ in

5 mm · ¼ in

2 cm · ¾ in

card

2 cm · ¾ in

2 mm · ½₂ in

2 mm · ½₂ in

hinge

tab

2 cm · ¾ in

tab

1 cm · ⅓ in

10 To line the lid, choose the same method as you used for lining the box. Using the internal dimensions which you noted earlier, cut paper-backed fabric or a lining card to this size. Cover the lining card with lining fabric if you have chosen to use this method.

When fully dry, open the box and glue the internal hinge flap in place, then glue in the lid lining which you have just prepared.

To cover the outside base, take the dimensions of the outside base, subtract 2 mm (¹⁄₁₂ in) from both measurements and cut paper-backed fabric or thin card to this size. Cover the latter, if using, with lining fabric. Glue in place. Alternatively, you could use a piece of felt as a base covering.

One of the traditional uses for a hinge-lidded box was for storing handkerchiefs. This one has been sized especially to fit a mansized handkerchief but could easily hold several smaller ladies' handkerchiefs and a lavender bag or used as a much more aesthetically pleasing container for paper tissues.

8 Insert the wadding, then glue down the top edge, pulling the fabric taut over the thin card, wadding and stiff card to give a neat front edge. At the corners, neaten with a point turner. Glue the tabs up (8), apply glue to each of the two sides in turn and pull the fabric flaps tautly into place as before.

9 To position the lid, glue the outside of the hinge side of the box. Place the lid down in position on the box and smooth the fabric hinge down onto the glued side (9). The

Separate lid

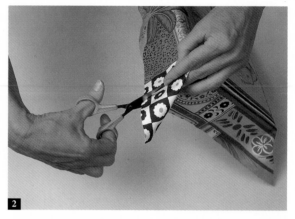

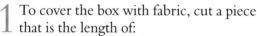

1 To cover the box with fabric, cut a piece that is the length of:
- the box circumference + 2 cm (¾ in)
and the width of:
- the height of the box + 3 cm (1¼ in)

Ensuring that there is a 1.5 cm (⅝ in) over-lap at the top and bottom, glue the fabric onto the box by wrapping it round the sides in the following order:

place 1 cm (⅜ in) onto one of the short sides, then long, short, long and finally the last short side. Neaten the final corner with a fold under if the fabric is thin enough **(1)**, or trim the excess fabric to fit the side exactly.

2 Deal with the excess fabric at the bottom and top of the box as described for the hinged lid (steps 2 and 3).

To line the box sides and bases, follow the instructions on pages 24 to 25.

3 Construct the box lid in the same way as the box (see page 17). If you wish to pad the lid, cut a piece of wadding to the exact size of the lid, glue the lid and press the wadding in place. Cut a piece of outer fabric that is the width of the lid plus four times the height plus 2 cm (¾ in) and the length of the lid plus four times the height plus 2 cm (¾ in).

For a padded lid: lay the outer fabric right side down. Paste glue to both long sides of the lid, then lay the lid, wadding side down, cen-trally on the fabric. Bring up one long side and press it in place along the entire length of

the box, then, pulling gently on the fabric to stretch it evenly over the padding, pull up onto the second long side and press in place.

For an unpadded lid: paste glue to the lid and place centrally on the fabric. Glue each of the long sides, pull the fabric up and press smoothly into place.

4 For both types of lid: cut all four corners to remove excess fabric **(2)**. Glue inside one long edge, fold the fabric over and press into place. Glue the excess fabric onto the base of the lid. Repeat for the other long side.

5 For the short sides, glue the entire width both inside and out, fold the fabric **(3)** and press into place, pulling the fabric tautly and evenly over the lid. Glue the excess fabric onto the base as before. Take the internal mea-surement of the lid and cut a piece of lining fabric to fit exactly. Glue into place.

I found a lovely printed fabric copy of a Victorian watercolour to use for the top of the box in which I keep inspirational garden-ing articles. I made a box to fit the design exactly, then mixed this fabric with a simple, two-coloured check. The lining is in a complementary, plain coloured, paper-backed fabric.

Digitalis sceptrum

Lining boxes

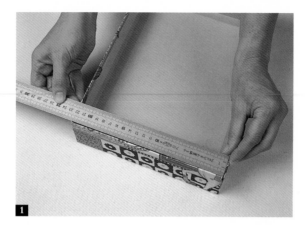

The decisions about whether and how to line a box will very much depend on what it is to be used for. There are three alternatives: no lining; lining with paper-backed fabric and lining with fabric-covered card. If the main purpose of the box is for visual impact or functional storage, you may prefer not to line it at all. Otherwise a simple lining with paper-backed fabric would suffice. This is a quick method but because of the limited range of colours available, you are restricted to plain colours. However, if the box is to be a gift or to be used for jewellery or handkerchiefs, it is pleasing to have as beautiful an interior as exterior finish. Although more time-consuming, the finish is much more professional and a wider range of alternative fabrics is available.

Lining with paper-backed fabric

Choose one side of the box and measure the internal width exactly (1). Measure the depth

and add 1 cm (³⁄₈ in). Draw this rectangle with a pencil on the reverse of the paper-backed fabric and cut out with a craft knife and ruler. Paste glue to the chosen side and a 1 cm (³⁄₈ in) strip on the base.

Position the fabric so that the top lies 2 mm (¹⁄₁₂ in) below the rim of the box and there is a 1 cm (³⁄₈ in) overlap onto the base. Press well into position (2).

Continue with an adjoining side ensuring that the level of the fabric at the top is consistent on all four sides and that each piece is well butted up to the previous side (3).

For the base, take the internal dimensions of the box, less 2 mm (¹⁄₁₂ in) on both length and width and cut out in paper-backed fabric. Check before glueing to ensure a neat fit, paste glue to the base and stick into place. Press well to ensure good adhesion.

Lining with lining cards

Using thin card, cut out four lining cards as follows:
inside height of the box less 2 mm (¹⁄₁₂ in) x inside width of the sides less 2 mm (¹⁄₁₂ in).

These cards can be covered in a variety of fabrics: paper-backed, contrasting or coordinating, plain or patterned.

Paste glue onto the card and cover with the chosen fabric, leaving a 1 cm (³⁄₈ in) overlap on all four sides. Cut away the excess fabric at the corners.

Glue the top flap down (4). Paste glue to the side on which you are working and a 1 cm

(⅜ in) strip on the base of the box, then a 1 cm (⅜ in) strip on both sides where the side overlaps will extend. Position the card, so that it lies 2 mm (1/12 in) below the rim of the box and press firmly into place not forgetting the base and side overlaps.

Take the piece of card for one of the adjoining sides, cover as before, glue down the top flap and this time glue down the side that will abut the overlap of the previous side. Before glueing always check that you have folded down the correct side. Glue this into place (5) and continue for side three.

On the last side, fold in the top and both sides and glue into place.

For the base, measure the internal dimensions of the box, less 2 mm (1/12 in) on length and width and cut out in card. Cover with lining fabric with a 1 cm (⅜ in) overlap all round. Clip across the corners to within 1 mm (1/16 in), fold and glue all sides down (for a detailed explanation of corners, see page 27). Glue into place and press firmly. It is a good idea to place weights in the box until the glue is completely dry.

Padding

By padding the top of a box, you can subtly alter its impact. Choose a suitable finish for the box you are making:
- a functional shoe box needs simply to be covered with fabric. It would be a waste of time to pad a box that will be stacked.
- decorative boxes, e.g. hat and gift boxes, can benefit from having their lids padded. This gives them a more luxurious feel.

Use polyester wadding of varying thicknesses, depending on the degree of "loft" you require but always choose a good quality, fairly dense padding. This can be bought by the metre or yard, then cut as you require it.

Cover the lid of the box with glue, press the wadding in place, trim to shape, then cover with the outer fabric (see page 22).

An alternative and more elaborate method of padding, but one that I think gives a more professional finish, is to sandwich the wadding between the card of the box lid and thin card. This technique is explained in the method for making a box with an attached lid (page 19).

Spines

The following traditional techniques concentrate on aspects of creating a folder or file. They are used in various projects throughout the book.

When making a folder, the spine gives the all-important rigidity and flexibility to the construction. It is, therefore, important to choose the right fabric. Paper-backed fabric or similar is ideal, and imitation leather or a very fine natural leather works well. Generally, cotton fabric is not strong enough.

The following method details how to make the spine of a folder measuring 24 x 32 cm (9½ x 12½ in), with a 3.5 cm (1⅓ in) overlap front and back and a 2.5 cm (1 in) gusset.

Take a piece of paper-backed fabric, 36 x 9.5 cm (13¾ x 3¾ in) which will become the outer spine. Draw two pencil lines the length of the piece, both 3.5 cm (1½ in) in from the outer edges. Now draw a horizontal line 2 cm (¾ in) down from the top edge. This gives you guidelines for the placing of the front and back sides of the folder (1).

Paste glue along the length of one of the 3.5 cm (1½ in) strips. Take one of the prepared folder sides and line up with your pencil marks. Turn over and press. Repeat for the

other side, checking that it aligns exactly with the other side (2). Paste glue to the 2 cm (¾ in) overlaps at top and bottom , fold over and press into place.

Cut a piece of paper-backed fabric 31.8 x 5.5 cm (12⅜ x 2¼ in). This is the inner spine. Paste glue to the reverse of this piece and position centrally to cover the gap between front and back covers (3). Press firmly and at this stage, do not fold your work but leave it flat and well weighted until completely dry.

Corners

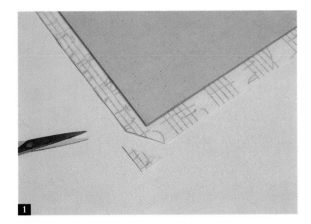

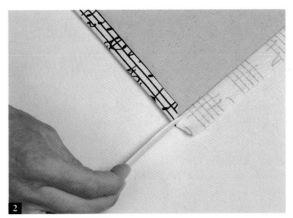

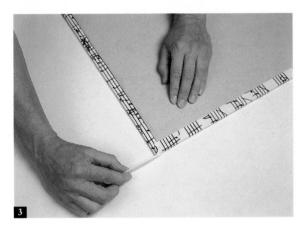

Making a flat corner

This method describes how to turn over the fabric overlaps on stiff or thin card at the corners to obtain a neat, sharp finish.

Paste glue to the card and cover with fabric, leaving a 1.5 cm (⅝ in) overlap on all sides. Trim across the corner at an angle (1). This removes excess fabric that would otherwise make the corner too bulky. The gap between the cut and the card will depend on the thickness of the card but is usually at least the same as the thickness of the card.

Paste a border of glue along one edge of the card, fold the fabric overlap onto this edge with a point turner and press firmly. With the point turner, pinch the fabric overlap at the corner so that the fold in the excess fabric is flattened (2).

Paste a border of glue onto the second side and fold the fabric over, again using the point turner to flatten the fabric against the card (3). Turn over and check that the corner is neat: at this stage, when the glue is not yet dry, a corner can be neatened considerably by the use of the point turner.

Contrast corners

Contrast corners

Contrast corners, as seen on the concertina file (page 80) or the correspondence folder (page 99), are dealt with in a similar way. They can be made to any size and, indeed, in any fabric. There are two possible methods: one using paper-backed fabric and the other using a lining fabric over thin card. Both methods follow and each are based on a 5 cm (2 in) corner for a covered piece of card.

In paper-backed fabric

Add 1.5 cm ($\frac{5}{8}$ in) to the measurement and cut out a 6.5 cm ($2\frac{5}{8}$ in) square. Cut in half diagonally to make two corner pieces. Position one of the corners against the card, so that there is a 1.5 cm ($\frac{5}{8}$ in) overlap on two sides. Pencil round the corner, thus making a triangle which should be covered with glue. Reposition the corner on the outside of the card, press firmly in position, trim the corner and glue as for a flat corner (1).

In contrast fabric

This method avoids any frayed edges which might result from using the above method with a lining rather than paper-backed fabric and which would spoil your work. Using thin card, cut out a 5 cm (2 in) square and cut in half as above. Glue and cover with your chosen fabric, so that there is a 1.5 cm ($\frac{5}{8}$ in) overlap on all three sides. Cut across the right-angled corner to within 2 mm ($\frac{1}{12}$ in) of the card. Fold the long edge over and glue down. Now glue the whole of the card triangle and position it exactly on the outside corner (2). Finally, fold and glue the two remaining over-laps as for a flat corner.

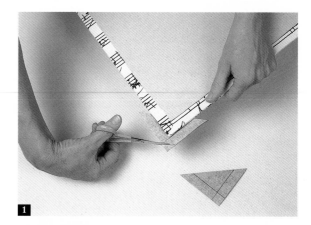

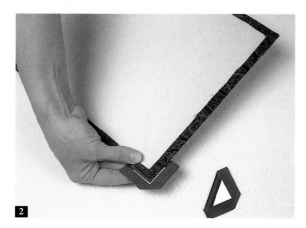

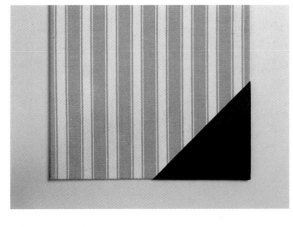

Six different corner finishes on the same base fabric show you how much the attention to detail matters and how radically they can alter the finished appearance.

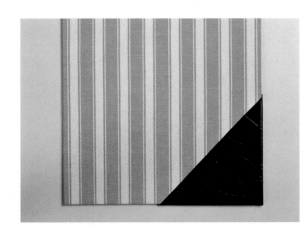

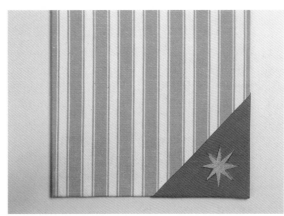

Divisions

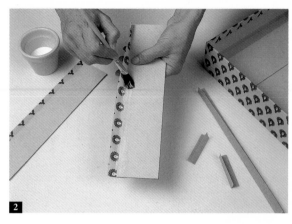

Occasionally a box will need to have its internal space divided into sections (see, for example, the cutlery box on page 89). The principle is very simple and can be adapted to make any number or shape of divisions.

1 Mark the position of the required divisions with a pencil on the base card of the box before construction.

2 Construct the box as usual, ensuring that the pencil markings are on the inside of the box (1).

3 Measure the internal height of the box and subtract 2 mm (1/12 in) to calculate the height of the dividing card. Measure the internal length of the required division for its length. Cut out in stiff card and check the fit. It is important that the card is not such an exact fit that it distorts the shape of the box.

4 To make an attractive finish, it is a good idea to make the top of the dividing card contrast with the actual box lining. For example, choose the outer fabric to cover the top of the dividers, then cover the lining cards in contrast/plain fabric. Cut a strip of fabric the exact length of the divider and 2 cm (3/4 in) wide. Glue this evenly over the top edge of the divider (2).

5 Using kraft paper, kraft the division in place (see page 17) with strips along the base and sides and on each side of the division, checking with a set square that the card is vertical (3).

6 Line each resulting divided area with paper-backed fabric or lining cards.

Remember that for each division you make, you double the number of lining cards needed to complete the work, so for example, one central division will mean two sets of four lining cards for the sides and two for the bases.

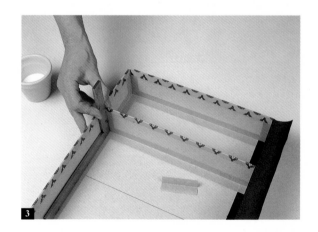

Pencil Pot

A pencil pot is an easy introduction to cartonnage and makes a very useful container.

MAKING UP

1 Construct the box as described in the basic box instructions on page 17. Use a sandpaper block to level the top edges (1).

2 Press the fabric to remove any creases. Starting at one corner of the box, paste a 1 cm (¾ in) border of glue down one side and position one short end of the fabric over this border, keeping an equal overlap of fabric at both top and bottom.

3 Keeping the fabric taut and the pattern straight, glue each side in turn and press the fabric into place. Neaten the final corner with a fold under if the fabric is thin enough and an accurately cut edge if it is too thick to make a neat fold. Glue down and wipe off any excess glue with a damp cloth (2). At each top corner remove the excess fabric as described on page 18 (step 3). Glue the resulting four flaps down inside the box. Use the turner to give a neat finish to the corners. Cut and glue the corners at the base in the same way.

4 Cut the paper-backed fabric into four side pieces, an inside and an outside base as follows. Checking each piece against the relevant side and trimming where necessary, paste one inside side of the pot and place the paper-backed fabric over. Position the piece so that it sits 2 mm (¹⁄₁₂ in) below the top edge and runs onto the base. Use the turner to make a crisp edge at the inside base of the pot. Finger press to secure (3).

5 Repeat with the other three sides, then the inner and finally the outer base (4).

Wine box

MATERIALS

stiff card: 32 x 64 cm
  (13 x 25 in)
outer fabric: 35 x 77 cm
  (14 x 31 in)
paper-backed fabric:
  33 x 51 cm (13 x 20 in)
kraft paper strips

Pieces required
stiff card
box adjacent sides:
  32 x 10.9 cm
  (12 $7/12$ x 4 $1/4$ in) – cut two
box upper sides:
  31.8 x 9.5 cm
  (12 $1/2$ x 4 $1/4$ in) – cut two
box base: 9.5 x 10.9 cm
  (3 $3/4$ x 4 $1/4$ in) – cut one
lid adjacent sides:
  11.7 x 4.5 cm
  (4 $5/8$ x 1 $3/4$ in)– cut two
lid upper sides: 10.3 x 4.3 cm
  (4 $9/16$ x 1 $11/16$ in) – cut two
lid base:10.3 x 11.7 cm
  (4 $9/16$ x 4 $5/8$ in) – cut one

outer fabric
box: 35 x 46 cm
  (13 $3/4$ x 18 in) – cut one
lid: 31.5 x 30.5 cm
  (12 $3/8$ x 12 in) – cut one

paper-backed fabric
insides: 33 x 10.5 cm
  (13 x 4 $1/8$ in) – cut two
  33 x 9.5 cm (13 x 3 $3/4$ in)
  – cut two
lid: 9.5 x 10.5 cm
  (3 $3/4$ x 4 $1/8$ in) – cut one
base: 9.5 x 10.5 cm
  (3 $3/4$ x 4 $1/8$ in) – cut two

PREPARATION

Cut out and label the stiff
card, outer and paper-
backed fabric following the
cutting plans opposite and
on page 34.

MAKING UP

Construct the box as
described in the basic box
instructions on page 17 and
the lid following the
variation given for a separate
lid on page 22. This box is
lined with paper-backed
fabric only.

WINE BOX

Stiff card

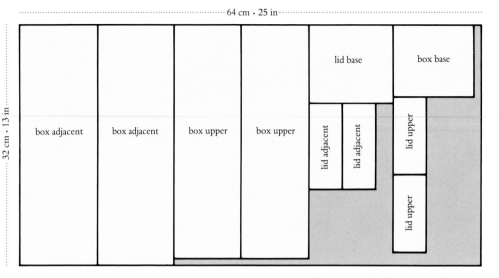

Outer fabric

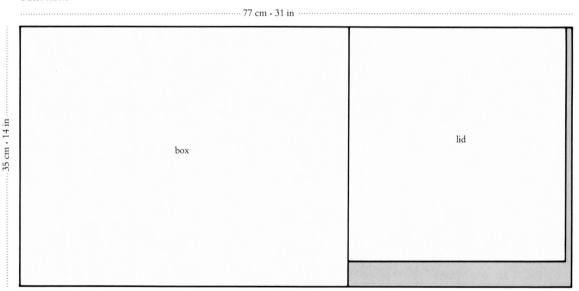

Personalize your bottle gift
with a fabric-covered wine
or spirit box. Try to find an
individual fabric with a
print or design particularly
suited to the recipient.

Book box

To fit a book measuring
12 x 17.5 x 2.5 cm
(4¾ x 6⅞ x 1 in)

MATERIALS

stiff card: 30 x 22 cm
  (12 x 9 in)
outer and lining paper:
  44 x 33 cm (18 x 13 in)
kraft paper strips

Pieces required
stiff card
adjacent sides: 13 x 18 cm
  (5⅛ x 7¹/₁₆ in) – cut two
upper sides: 12.8 x 3.1 cm
  (5 x 1¼ in) – cut two
base: 3.1 x 18 cm
  (1¼ x 7¹/₁₆ in) – cut one

outer and lining paper
outside: 44 x 15 cm
  (17⅜ x 6 in) – cut one
adjacent insides:
  12.5 x 17.6 cm
  (4¹⁵/₁₆ x 6¹⁵/₁₆ in) – cut two
upper insides: 12.5 x 3 cm
  (4¹⁵/₁₆ x 1¼ in) – cut two
outer base: 18 x 3.5 cm
  (7¹/₁₆ x 1⅜ in) – cut one

PREPARATION
Cut out and label the stiff
card, outer and lining paper
following the cutting plans
opposite.

MAKING UP
This box shows paper as an
alternative covering to fabric.
It is used both on the outside
and inside of the box,
although the inside base is
left unlined. Use a coin to
draw the shape of the finger
recesses in the middle of one
side of the top and bottom
pieces of the box. Cut out,
then continue to construct
the box as described in the
basic box instructions on
page 17.

WINE BOX continued

Paper-backed fabric

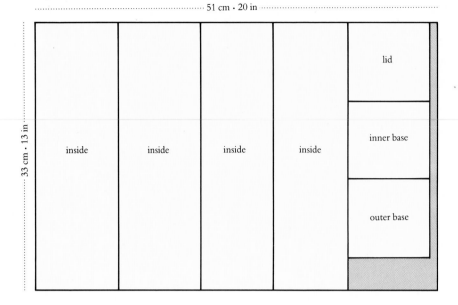

BOOK BOX

Stiff card

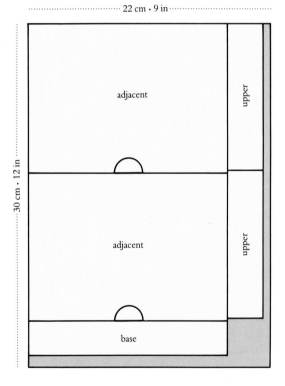

Outer and lining paper

Give an antique book, first
edition print or commemo-
rative photograph album in
a specially-made box.

Card box

MATERIALS
stiff card: 27 x 36 cm
  (11 x 15 in)
outer fabric: 21 x 58 cm
  (9 x 23 in)
paper-backed fabric:
  6 x 13 cm (3 x 6 in)
kraft paper strips

Pieces required
stiff card
box adjacent sides:
  13.5 x 18 cm (5 ⁵⁄₁₆ x 7 ¹⁄₁₆ in)
  – cut two
box upper sides:
  3.1 x 17.8 cm (1 ¼ x 7 in)
  – cut two
box base: 3.1 x 13.5 cm
  (1 ¼ x 5 ⁵⁄₁₆ in) – cut one
lid adjacent sides:
  2.5 x 14.2 cm (1 x 5 ⅝ in)
  – cut two
lid upper sides: 2.3 x 3.8 cm
  (⅞ x 1 ½ in) – cut two
lid base: 3.8 x 14.2 cm
  (1 ½ x 5 ⅝ in) – cut one

outer fabric
box: 21 x 36 cm
  (8 ¼ x 14 ⅛ in) – cut one
lid: 12 x 22 cm (4 ¾ x 8 ¾ in)
  – cut one

paper-backed fabric
lid and base: 3 x 13 cm
  (1 ¼ x 5 ⅛ in) – cut two

PREPARATION
Cut out and label the stiff
card, outer and paper-backed
fabric following the cutting
plans opposite.

MAKING UP
Construct the box as
described in the basic box
instructions on page 17 and
the lid following the
variation given for a separate
lid on page 22. This box is
lined with paper-backed
fabric just on the inner lid
and outer base.

**Cards and notelets make
lovely presents and even
more so when you also
make the gift box for them.**

Stiff card

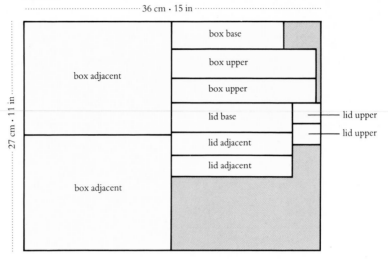

Outer fabric

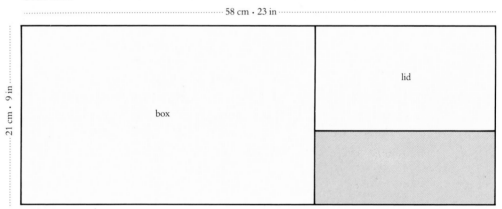

Paper-backed fabric

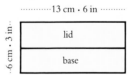

The
DRESSING
ROOM

One of my most difficult tasks as an interior designer over the years has been to find a way to organize clients' dressing rooms economically.

When I was introduced to cartonnage, one of the first items I designed, in preference to more decorative pieces, was a storage box. Boxes for papers and filing were soon developed and after these came boxes for shoes and boots, socks, seasonal sports gear and little-worn party clothes and accessories.

My first dressing room commission was for forty shoe boxes – and all in the same fabric!

For my own dressing area I have used a mixture of fabrics – linen with a smart navy edge and a country check in soft green for shoes and boots, and a green stripe for scarves, belts, costume jewellery and lingerie.

These, together with hat boxes and shirt boxes, soft bags in country fabrics, some small trays for day-to-day storage, complete the organization of my wardrobe – in just a few weeks you could do the same for yours!

Hat Box

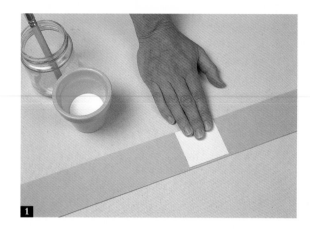

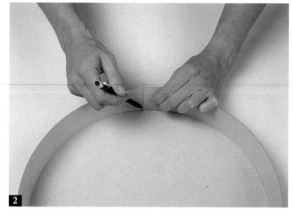

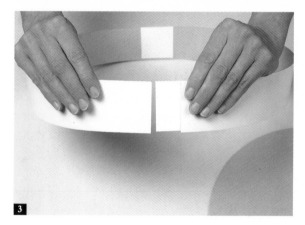

TOOLS
1 cm (⅜ in) flat glue brush
2 cm (¾ in) flat glue brush
glue
point turner
scissors
cutting mat
steel ruler
set square
craft knife
pencil

MATERIALS
stiff card: 35 x 70 cm
  (14 x 28 in)
thin card: 70 x 91 cm
  (28 x 36 in)
outer fabric: 115 x 85 cm
  (46 x 34 in)
paper-backed fabric:
  115 x 62 cm (46 x 25 in)
kraft paper
wadding (optional)
ribbon or braid: 1.15m
  (1¼ yds) long, 15 mm
  (½ in) wide and 1.15m
  (1¼ yds) long, 7 mm
  (¼ in) wide

Pieces required
stiff card
lid circle: 35 cm (13¾ in)
  diameter – cut one
base circle: 34.5 cm (13⁷⁄₁₂ in)
  diameter – cut one

thin card
lid sides: 6 x 56 cm
  (2⅜ x 22 in) – cut two
base sides: 22.5 x 55 cm
  (8⅞ x 21⅝ in) – cut two
base joiner cards:
  10 x 22.2 cm
  (3¹⁵⁄₁₆ x 8¾ in) – cut two
lid joiner cards: 5.7 x 6 cm
  (2¼ x 2⅜ in) – cut two
lid circle: 34.5 cm (13⁷⁄₁₂ in)
  diameter – cut one
base circle: 34 cm (13⅜ in)
  diameter – cut one

outer fabric
lid sides: 115 x 20 cm
  (45¼ x 8 in) – cut one
base sides: 115 x 26 cm
  (45¼ x 10¼ in) – cut one
lid circle: 39 cm (15½ in)
  diameter – cut one

Continued on page 42

MAKING UP

1 To make the lid, take the two narrow strips of card that make up the lid rim and place side by side to make one long strip. Cut a piece of kraft paper 6 cm (2½ in) wide and 6 cm (2½ in) long. Glue this centrally over the join - this will be the outside of the lid. Turn over, being careful not to dislodge the join. Take one of the joiner cards and cover one side with glue. Place this centrally over the join so that one end is flush with the card strip and there is a 3 mm (⅛ in) gap at the other end **(1)**.

Leave to dry, then fold this long strip tightly round the lid base. Mark with a pencil line where the card overlaps **(2)**. Cut off the excess card.

Now take the second joiner card and mark with a pencil the centre vertical line. Glue one half of the joiner card and fix to one of the free ends of the rim strip, ensuring that it is on the same side of the rim as the previous joiner card and that the 3 mm (⅛ in) gap is along the same edge. Leave to dry.

2 Paste glue to the remaining half of the joiner card and glue the free end in place, so that both sides abut to make a circle **(3)**. Secure on the outside with a piece of kraft paper 6 cm (2½ in) wide and 6 cm (2½ in) long. Leave to dry, then glue the entire circumference of the lid card and place on a flat surface. Hold the lid rim so that the edge with

the joiner card gaps is at the bottom, then lower the circle over the lid card and gently apply pressure round the base to glue the two pieces together. Leave until completely dry.

To increase the strength of the join, glue small folded strips of kraft paper on the inside between the lid and the rim.

For a padded lid, put four or five dabs of glue onto the top of the lid and press on the wadding. Trim to the exact shape of the lid.

3 Take the piece of outer fabric for the lid and cut "V" shapes at regular intervals all round the circumference no deeper than 1 cm (⅜ in). Put four spots of glue on the compass points of the lid sides, place the fabric centrally onto the lid and fix down to the glue spots, pulling the fabric until taut but not ruckled **(4)**. Make another four fixing points in between these and continue the process. Glue the rest of the lid side and stick down.

I don't think hat boxes have ever been as popular as at present - not only for their designated use but also as decorative storage for all sorts of things - boxes designed to be on show, not hidden in a cupboard. All kinds of boxes to paint and to cover with paper are available in stores, but fabric coverings both inside and outside give a softer, more luxurious finish and do look special.

Use these round boxes for needlepoint and knitting wools in the sitting room, napkins in the dining room, towels in the bathroom, and a myriad other uses to suit your own needs. They can be covered in almost any fabric, decorated with applied and stencilled motifs, or even personal messages hand written onto the fabric, and finished with a wide variety of trimmings.

41

Continued from page 40

paper-backed fabric
base sides: 115 x 24 cm
  (45 ¼ x 9 ½ in) - cut one
lid circle: 38 cm (15 in)
  diameter - cut one
inner base circle: 37 cm
  (14 ½ in) diameter - cut one
outer base circle: 34 cm
  (13 ½ in) diameter - cut one

PREPARATION
Cut out the lid and base
circles in stiff card using the
templates given on the folded
sheet at the back of the book.
Use the card as a template to
cut the other circles required,
increasing or reducing the
diameter as necessary. Cut
and label the remaining
pieces in stiff and thin card,
outer and paper-backed
fabric following the cutting
plans on page 44.

4

5

Glue approximately one quarter of the outside rim and place the fabric for the lid with
the right side against the glued rim and one
long, raw edge exactly lined up with the
bottom of the lid rim (5). Ensuring that the
short end of the fabric you are starting with is
square, press carefully in place, then continue
glueing and fixing all round the rim. Where
the fabric overlaps, trim back to 1 cm (⅜ in),
glue and press down lightly.

When dry, glue the inside of the rim, fold
the fabric over to the inside, pull firmly and
press down neatly. Glue the overlap onto the
base of the lid, clipping as necessary.

4 Check that the circle of lid lining card fits
easily in the lid. Glue one side and cover
with the lining fabric circle. Clip the edges ,
fold over and glue down, then glue the lining
into the lid. Leave under weights to dry.

5 To make the base, take the two strips of
base card and proceed exactly as for the lid
(step 1), using kraft strips 6 x 22.5 cm
(2 ½ x 8 ⅞ in) and joiner cards 10 x 22.2 cm
(3 ¹⁵⁄₁₆ x 8 ¾ in). Now cover the entire inside
length of this strip with paper-backed fabric,
so that the top rim is flush with the card;
there is a 1.5 cm (⅝ in) overlap on the
opposite long side; the side with the half
joiner card has a 1 cm (⅜ in) overlap and the
other short side is flush with the card.

When glueing, leave a 1 cm (⅜ in) strip
along the bottom where the paper-backed
fabric is not glued - this is where the base will
be inserted. Where the paper-backed fabric
overlaps on this side, clip "V"s all along the
length to within 2 mm (¹⁄₁₂ in) of the card.

6 Now cover the outside with fabric, so that
there is an equal overlap at top and
bottom and at each of the sides (6). Be careful
to keep the fabric straight at all times and
smooth out any creases or bubbles. It is generally easier to glue a quarter of the side and
apply the fabric rather than paste the whole
side at once.

At the half joint end, where the joiner card
is already fixed, glue the fabric over the end of
the box and flat onto the joiner piece. Use a
point turner to push the fabric tightly into the

6

7

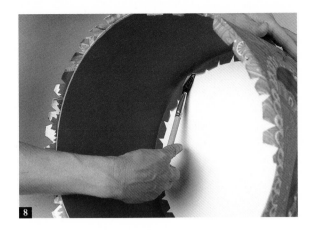

angle made by the joiner piece and the card (7). Paste glue to the remaining half of the joiner piece (covered with fabric).

Roll the box side so that the card ends meet, with the fabric overlap on the outside. Press the glued joiner card against the inside of the card and hold in place until firmly stuck. Lightly glue the wrong side of the remaining 1 cm (⅜ in) fabric overlap and finger press neatly in place over the join.

On the inside, glue the paper-backed fabric overlap and press into place. Put the joint under weights and leave to dry.

7 When dry, turn the cylinder upside down and gently push the lining flaps a little way into the box. Glue the entire circumference of the box base and slip it into position. Turn the box over and leave it to dry. Then, in order to strengthen this join, glue the lining overlaps onto the inner base of the box (8) and the fabric overlaps onto the outer base.

Cover the outer base with the relevant circle of paper-backed fabric (9).

For the inner base, check that the thin card circle fits easily into the base, then cover with paper-backed fabric and glue into the bottom of the box.

8 At the top of the box, fold the excess fabric over onto the inside and carefully glue into place. Glue the ribbon or braid in place to cover the join between lining and outer fabric (10), using clothes pegs to hold the ribbon in place until dry (11).

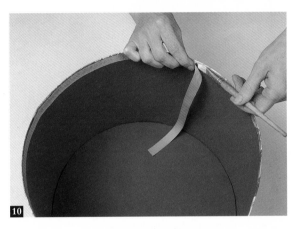

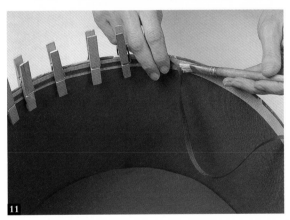

Large Hat Box

MATERIALS

stiff card: 101 x 51 cm
   (40 x 20 in)
thin card: 100 x 103 cm
   (40 x 41 in)
outer fabric: 99 x 165 cm
   (40 x 65 in)
paper-backed fabric:
   165 x 76 cm (65 x 30 in)
kraft paper
wadding (optional)
ribbon or braid: 1.65m
   (2 yds) long, 15 mm
   (½ in) wide and 1.65m
   (2 yds) long, 7 mm (¼ in)
   wide

Pieces required
stiff card
lid circle: 51 cm (20 in)
   diameter – cut one
base circle: 49.5 cm (19½ in)
   diameter – cut one

thin card
lid sides: 82 x 6 cm
   (32¼ x 2½ in) – cut two
base sides: 80 x 20 cm
   (31½ x 8 in) – cut two
base joiner cards:
   19.7 x 10 cm (7⅞ x 4 in)
   – cut two
lid joiner cards: 5.7 x 6 cm
   (2⅜ x 2½ in) – cut two
lid circle: 50.5 cm (19⅞ in)
   diameter – cut one
base circle: 49 cm (19¼ in)
   diameter – cut one

outer fabric
lid sides: 20 x 165 cm
   (8 x 65 in) – cut one
base sides: 24 x 165 cm
   (9½ x 65 in) – cut one
lid circle: 55 cm (21¾ in)
   diameter – cut one

Continued on page 45

LARGE HAT BOX

Paper-backed fabric
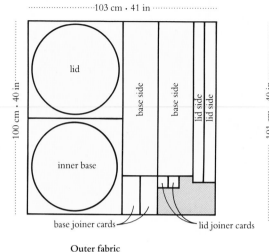

Thin card

Stiff card
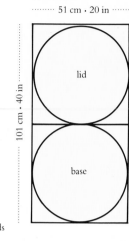

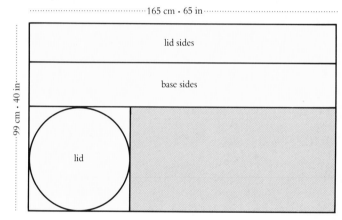

Outer fabric

HAT BOX

Thin card
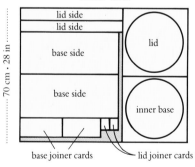

Stiff card
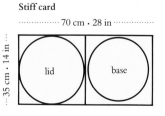

Outer fabric
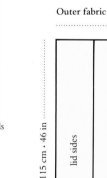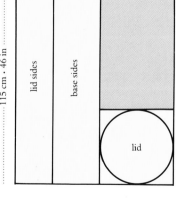

Paper-backed fabric
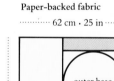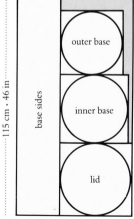

Continued from page 44

paper-backed fabric
base sides: 165 x 22 cm
 (65 x 8¾ in) – cut one
lid circle: 54 cm (21¼ in)
 diameter – cut one
inner base circle: 53 cm
 (20⅞ in) diameter
 – cut one
outer base circle: 49.5 cm
 (19½ in) diameter
 – cut one

PREPARATION
Use compasses to draw the
templates for the lid and base
circles, then cut out pieces as
required. Cut and label the
remaining pieces in stiff and
thin card, outer and paper-
backed fabric following the
cutting plans on page 44.

MAKING UP
Construct this larger box as
described in the instructions
on pages 40 to 43.

We adapted the basic
round hat box to accom-
modate top hats and bowler
hats worn occasionally and
needing strong storage in
between. We chose an
Italian hand-printed cotton
check, but you could use a
wool worsted family tartan
for a Scottish friend or one
of the many traditional
plaids, just because you like
the colours.

It is almost impossible to find decorative boxes in which to store large-brimmed hats. Lovely, extravagant, but seldom worn, hats for special occasions are often vulnerable to damage and need to be well protected between outings.

We have given measurements for a box to take an average size of hat on page 40 but you can adapt both the diameter and the height to suit your hat.

Shoe Box

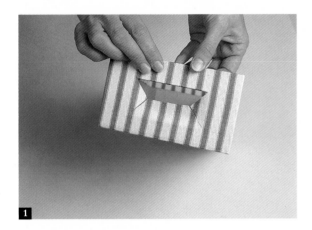

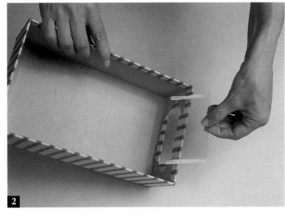

MAKING UP

1 Cut a rectangular opening in one of the upper sides as follows:

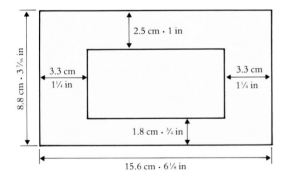

2.5 cm · 1 in

8.8 cm · 3⁷⁄₁₆ in

3.3 cm
1¼ in

3.3 cm
1¼ in

1.8 cm · ¾ in

15.6 cm · 6⅛ in

2 Assemble the box following the method described on page 17 and the lid following the method on page 22.

3 To cover the lid with fabric, follow the instructions on page 22 omitting the padding. To cover the box with fabric, follow the same instructions, then where the fabric covers the rectangular opening, cut a diagonal cross in the fabric (1) and trim the flaps of fabric to 1.5 cm (⅝ in) in width. Fold the flaps onto the inside and glue down.

4 Line with paper-backed fabric as described on page 24. Take the window side as the first side and place the relevant piece of paper-backed fabric in position inside the box, placing it 2 mm (¹⁄₁₂ in) below the

rim, then from the outside, trace the window opening onto the reverse of the paper-backed fabric. Remove the fabric and enlarge the pencilled shape by 1 mm (¹⁄₁₆ in) all round, then cut the centre out.

Glue in the piece of perspex (2), then cover with the lining piece (3). Continue to line the other three sides and the inside base, then cover the outside base with a further piece of paper-backed fabric or felt as required.

TOOLS
1 cm (⅜ in) flat glue brush
2 cm (¾ in) flat glue brush
glue
point turner
scissors
cutting mat
steel ruler
set square
craft knife
pencil

MATERIALS
stiff card: 34 x 75 cm
 (14 x 30 in)
outer fabric: 43 x 95 cm
 (17 x 38 in)
paper-backed fabric:
 28 x 87 cm (11 x 35 in)
perspex: 7 x 11 cm
 (2¾ x 4¼ in)
kraft paper strips

Pieces required
stiff card
box adjacent sides: 9 x 28 cm
 (3½ x 11 in) – cut two
box upper sides:
 15.6 x 8.8 cm
 (6⅛ x 3⁷⁄₁₆ in) – cut two
box base: 15.6 x 28 cm
 (6⅛ x 11 in) – cut one
lid adjacent sides:
 28.7 x 2.7 cm
 (11¼ x 1¹⁄₁₆ in) – cut two
lid upper sides: 2.5 x 16.3 cm
 (1 x 6⁵⁄₁₂) – cut two
lid base: 28.7 x 16.3 cm
 (11¼ x 6⁵⁄₁₂) – cut one

outer fabric
outside: 12 x 95 cm
 (4¾ x 38 in) – cut one
lid: 31 x 43 cm (12¼ x 17 in)
 – cut one

paper-backed fabric
adjacent sides: 28 x 10 cm
 (11 x 4 in) – cut two
upper sides: 15.5 x 10 cm
 (6¼ x 4 in) – cut two
base: 28 x 15.5 cm
 (11 x 6¼ in) – cut two
lid: 28 x 15.5 cm
 (11 x 6¼ in) – cut one

PREPARATION
Cut out and label all the pieces in stiff and thin card, perspex and paper-backed fabric following the cutting plans on page 49.

We adapted our basic storage box for the specific storage of shoes, which are always a problem especially with party wear and out-of-season styles.

At one end of the box there is a cut-out with a perspex cover, so that the contents can be viewed instantly, saving several hours writing labels or removing lids to find that vital pair.

This type of box is also very useful for storing photographs, or the measurements could be adapted for video cassettes, CDs and computer discs.

SHOE BOX

Stiff card

75 cm · 30 in

34 cm · 14 in

box adjacent

box adjacent

lid upper

lid upper

lid adjacent

lid adjacent

box base

box upper

box upper

lid base

Outer fabric

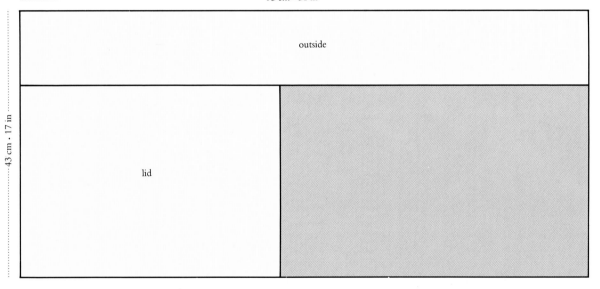

95 cm · 38 in

43 cm · 17 in

outside

lid

Paper-backed fabric

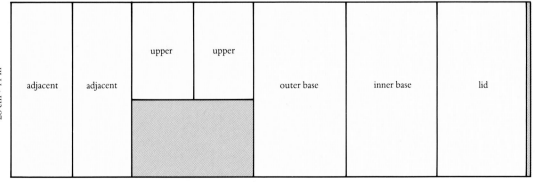

87 cm . 35 in

28 cm · 11 in

adjacent

adjacent

upper

upper

outer base

inner base

lid

This shirt box is made exactly as described on pages 17 and 22 for the basic box with a separate lid, to the measurements given opposite, and lined with paper-backed fabric. It could also be used to store shorts, scarves, belts and many other personal effects in the wardrobe or elsewhere.

SHIRT BOX

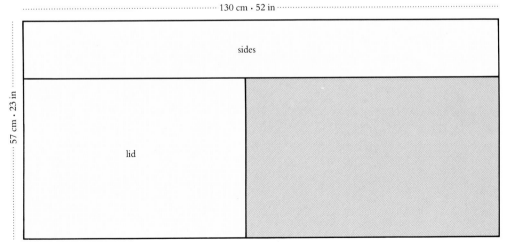

Stiff card

80 cm · 32 in

52 cm · 21 in

lid adjacent
lid adjacent
lid
box adjacent
box adjacent
box base

lid upper
lid upper
box upper
box upper

Paper-backed fabric

75 cm · 30 in

67 cm · 27 in

outer base
inner base
lid base

adjacent
upper

adjacent
upper

Outer fabric

130 cm · 52 in

57 cm · 23 in

sides

lid

Shirt Box

MATERIALS

stiff card: 52 x 80 cm
 (21 x 32 in)
outer fabric: 57 x 130 cm
 (23 x 52 in)
paper-backed fabric:
 67 x 75 cm (27 x 30 in)
kraft paper strips

Pieces required
stiff card
box adjacent sides:
 40 x 12 cm (16 x 4¾ in)
 – cut two
box upper sides:
 23.6 x 11.8 cm
 (9¼ x 4⅝ in) – cut two
box base: 40 x 23.6 cm
 (16 x 9¼ in) – cut one
lid top: 40.7 x 24.3 cm
 (16¼ x 9⁷⁄₁₂ in) – cut one
lid adjacent sides:
 40.7 x 4 cm
 (16⅛ x 1⁷⁄₁₂ in) – cut two
lid upper sides:
 3.8 x 24.3 cm
 (1½ x 9⁷⁄₁₂ in) – cut two

outer fabric
sides: 15 x 130 cm
 (6 x 52 in) – cut one
lid: 42 x 60 cm
 (16½ x 23½ in) – cut one

paper-backed fabric
base: 41 x 25 cm
 (16¼ x 10 in) – cut three
adjacent sides: 13 x 40 cm
 (5⅛ x 16 in) – cut two
upper sides: 13 x 24 cm
 (5⅛ x 9½ in) – cut two

PREPARATION
Cut out and label all the
pieces in stiff card, outer and
paper-backed fabrics
following the cutting plans
on the left.

MAKING UP
Construct the box as
described in the basic box
instructions on page 17 and
the lids following the
variation given for a separate
lid on page 22. This box is
lined with paper-backed
fabric only.

The
DRESSING
TABLE

Dressing tables are almost always made to be a feminine and pretty feature within the overall room design but are particularly difficult to keep tidy.

I made for myself the prettiest tray with tied corners, based on an antique tray I had seen at an exhibition, to keep my hair-bands and slides in. Almost immediately a friend asked me for a cufflink tray for her husband. Not, as it happened, to keep his cufflinks in, but to hold his loose change, watch and the bits and pieces which are turned out of his pockets at the end of each day! The first one was in a smart black check and proved to be so useful that it is now a standard tray in our range Although we still call it a cufflink tray, I have more often seen it used on desks, in cupboards and on side tables, in every room in the house, filled with cards, pot pourri, soaps, bottles, pencils, make-up, hairclips, brushes or costume jewellery, to name but a few uses.

The elegant, scallop-topped detail added to our basic square box seemed perfect for bedroom storage. Photograph frames in mixed sizes and fabrics were made to fit special prints.

The creams and pale yellows, stronger yellows and soft terracottas in silks, organdies, lace and toile already in the bedroom, were balanced with the stylish stripes and checks used on the cartonnage accessories.

Designed for hair bands and beads, this tray is also useful for pens, pencils, bottles, make-up, jewellery, cards, as a sewing tray, to store embroidery threads or tapestry wools, birthday cards, or garden seed packets. Make a tray in your chosen fabrics to suit your hobby - or make one for a friend.

We chose an elegant silk stripe for the outer fabric and a tiny print in a toning colour for the lining.

Experiment with different fabrics - try a plain fabric outside and a contrast inside or a checked outer and striped inner, then tie bows in a strong contrasting colour to stand out or a soft one to blend in.

Dressing Table Tray

TOOLS

1 cm (³⁄₈ in) flat glue brush
2 cm (³⁄₄ in) flat glue brush
glue
point turner
scissors
cutting mat
steel ruler
set square
craft knife
pencil
eyelet maker and eyelets

MATERIALS

stiff card: 34 x 40 cm
  (14 x 16 in)
thin card: 50 x 55 cm
  (20 x 22 in)
outer fabric: 36 x 42 cm
  (15 x 17 in)
lining fabric: 50 x 55 cm
  (20 x 22 in)
ribbon: 2.4 m (2½ yds) long,
  7 mm (¼ in) wide

PREPARATION

Following the cutting plans
below, cut out the tray shape
in stiff card using the
template given on the folded
sheet at the back of the book
and score along the dotted
lines.
    Cut out and label the thin
card and the lining fabric
pieces using the appropriate
templates for the sides and
adding a turning allowance of
2 cm (³⁄₄ in) all round for the
fabric. The base rectangle
measures 15.8 x 21.8 cm
(6¼ x 8½ in). Cut out and
label one in thin card and one
in lining fabric adding the
same turning allowance.

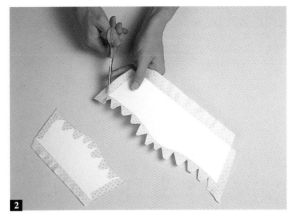

MAKING UP

1 Paste glue to the outside of the tray, i.e. the scored side, place centrally on the reverse of the outer fabric and press firmly. Trim the excess fabric round the shape, leaving an overlap of 1.5 cm (⁵⁄₈ in).

2 Clip into each corner, right up to the stiff card, then clip each curved side with a series of "V" shapes to within 2 mm (¹⁄₁₂ in) of the card. Paste a border of glue to the top of each inner side, fold over the excess fabric and press firmly into place (1).

3 Trim each thin card lining section down to fit neatly on the sides, then cover with lining fabric. Trim the lining fabric to a 1 cm (³⁄₈ in) overlap on the curved sides and 2 cm (³⁄₄ in) on the long straight base side.
    Clip the curved side as before and cut away

the excess fabric at the corners. Glue the clipped side and short sides down but leave the base flap free (2).

4 Glue each lining card into place but leave the base flaps free (3). When dry, hold the sides up at the angle you require, then glue the base flaps onto the base of the tray. Cover the thin base lining card with lining fabric. Glue in place and put under weights until dry.

5 Make three eyelet holes at each corner, thread ribbons through and tie to secure.

Stiff card and outer fabric

34 cm • 14 in

40 cm • 16 in

Thin card and lining fabric

50 cm • 20 in

55 cm • 22 in

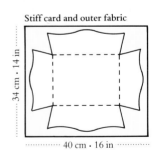

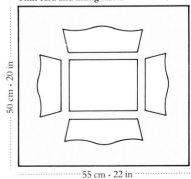

55

Scallop-Topped Box

TOOLS
1 cm (⅜ in) flat glue brush
2 cm (¾ in) flat glue brush
glue
point turner
scissors
cutting mat
steel ruler
set square
craft knife
pencil

MATERIALS
stiff card: 40 x 70 cm
  (16 x 28 in)
thin card: 40 x 70 cm
  (16 x 28 in)
outer fabric: 62 x 90 cm
  (25 x 36 in)
lining fabric: 50 x 81 cm
  (20 x 32 in)
kraft paper strips

Pieces required
stiff and thin card
adjacent sides: 9 x 22 cm
  (3½ x 8¾ in) – cut two
upper sides: 21.6 x 8.8 cm
  (8⁷⁄₁₂ x 3⁵⁄₁₂ in) – cut two
base: 21.6 x 22 cm
  (8⁷⁄₁₂ x 8¾ in) – cut one
lid: 30 x 30 cm
  (11¾ x 11¾ in) – cut one

outer fabric
box sides: 12 x 90 cm
  (4¾ x 35½ in) – cut one
base: 25 x 25 cm
  (10 x 10 in) – cut one
lid: 50 x 50 cm
  (19¾ x 19¾ in) – cut one

lining fabric
box sides: 25 x 14 cm
  (10 x 5½ in) – cut four
lid and base: 25 x 25 cm
  (10 x 10 in) – cut two
lid insides: 25 x 5 cm
  (10 x 2 in) – cut four

PREPARATION
For the base cut out and label
all the pieces in stiff and thin
card, outer and lining fabric
following the cutting plans
right and on page 58.
  Construct the base
following the instructions on
page 17 and lining with
fabric-covered card.

MAKING UP

1 Pencil a 22.3 x 22.3 cm (8⅞ x 8⅞ in) square in the centre of the stiff card lid piece, then, using the scallop template given on the folded sheet at the back of the book, draw this shape on each of the four sides. Cut out freehand. Score along the lines of the marked square, then fold the lid into shape and secure the corners both inside and out with kraft paper.

2 To cover, glue the top of the lid, then take a piece of the outer fabric measuring 50 x 50 cm (19½ x 19½ in) and place face down on the work surface. Place the lid centrally on the fabric, press, then turn over and smooth out any bubbles. Paste glue to one side of the lid and press the fabric down onto it, then repeat

on the opposite side. Trim the excess fabric on both sides to the scallop shape, leaving a 1 cm (⅜ in) overlap. At each end, trim the fabric so that there is a 1 cm (⅜ in) overlap onto the adjoining side.

  Clip the fabric round the curves (1), then glue down the fabric sections to the inside and the overlap onto the adjoining sides. Trim the excess fabric on the other two sides, so that the raw edge aligns exactly with the corner. Glue the inside lid, trim the fabric to the scallop shape, clip and stick down.

3 Cut lining cards for all four sides using the scallop template and cutting the thin card down to fit as necessary. Cut a lining card to fit inside the base of the lid. Cover all five pieces with lining fabric, clipping round the scallop shapes (2) and glue into place.

We have included a template for the scalloped edge in the back of the book, so that you can make this box easily. Please make sure that you use a very sharp knife to help you cut the regular scallops.

The box can be made in one design or in two complementary fabrics as here. These stripes look very elegant but if they are used, as here, against a plain box base, they will show up any unevenness in the scallop shape. So start with an all-over floral patterned fabric or a floral over a soft stripe, or a small stylized print, so that any slight errors will be disguised.

DOUBLE PHOTOGRAPH FRAME

Stiff card

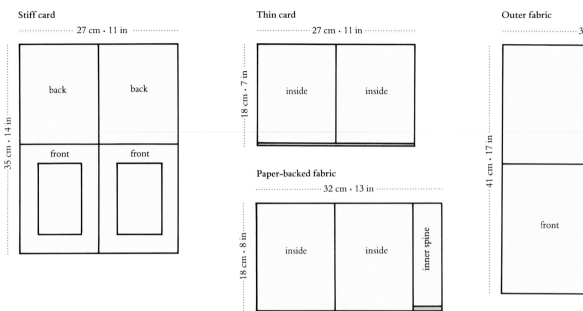

27 cm · 11 in

35 cm · 14 in

back   back

front   front

Thin card

27 cm · 11 in

18 cm · 7 in

inside   inside

Paper-backed fabric

32 cm · 13 in

18 cm · 8 in

inside   inside   inner spine

Outer fabric

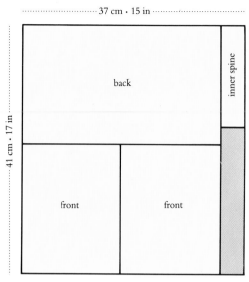

37 cm · 15 in

41 cm · 17 in

back   inner spine

front   front

SCALLOP-TOPPED BOX

Stiff and thin card

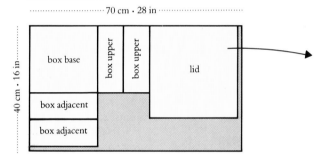

70 cm · 28 in

40 cm · 16 in

box base   box upper   box upper   lid

box adjacent

box adjacent

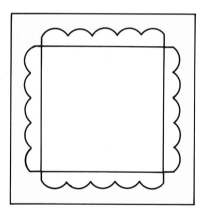

Outer fabric

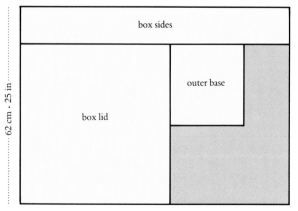

90 cm · 36 in

62 cm · 25 in

box sides

outer base

box lid

Lining fabric

81 cm · 32 in

50 cm · 20 in

inner lid   box upper   box upper   box adjacent   box adjacent

inner base   lid insides

Double Photograph Frame

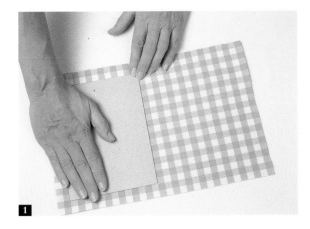

MAKING UP

1 Take the large piece of outer fabric and lay it face down on the work surface. Glue the two pieces of whole card for the backs and lay them centrally on the fabric with a 2 cm (¾ in) gap between them (1). Check with a ruler to ensure that the card pieces are exactly aligned (2).

Glue the reverse of the paper-backed fabric spine and stick this centrally over the gap between the cards (3). Trim the excess fabric at the corners to within 2 mm (¹⁄₁₂ in), then fold over and glue the top and bottom fabric overlaps. Repeat for the side overlaps. Take the outer fabric spine and glue this over the paper-backed fabric spine.

2 Take one of the two pieces of thin card and cover with paper-backed fabric, so that three of the sides are exactly aligned and there is an overlap of 5 mm (½ in) on the remaining short side. Trim any excess on the three aligning sides (4). Fold the overlap to the back of the card and glue.

Glue the pieces of stiff card for the frame fronts and lay centrally on the corresponding pieces of outer fabric. Press firmly.

TOOLS

1 cm (³⁄₈ in) flat glue brush
2 cm (¾ in) flat glue brush
glue
point turner
scissors
cutting mat
steel ruler
set square
craft knife
pencil

MATERIALS

stiff card: 35 x 27 cm
  (14 x 11 in)
thin card: 18 x 27 cm
  (7 x 11 in)
outer fabric: 41 x 37 cm
  (17 x 15 in)
paper-backed fabric:
  18 x 32 cm (8 x 13 in)

Pieces required
stiff card
backs: 17.5 x 13.5 cm
  (7 x 5 ½ in) – cut two
fronts: 17.5 x 13.5 cm
  (7 x 5 ½ in) – cut two

thin card
insides: 17.5 x 13.5 cm
  (7 x 5 ½ in) – cut two

outer fabric
back: 20.5 x 33 cm
  (8 ½ x 13 ½ in) – cut one
fronts: 20.5 x 16.5 cm
  (8 ½ x 6 ¾ in) – cut two
inner spine: 17.5 x 4 cm
  (7 x 1 ½ in) – cut one

paper-backed fabric
insides: 18 x 13.5 cm
  (7 ½ x 5 ½ in) – cut two
inner spine: 17.5 x 5 cm
  (7 x 2 in) – cut one

PREPARATION

Cut out and label all the pieces in stiff and thin card, outer and paper-backed fabric following the cutting plans on page 58. Cut out the central opening of the two fronts in stiff card, leaving a 3 cm (1 ¼ in) border all round.

We are asked more and more frequently for different designs of photograph frames, so we have shown a basic double frame here, with an alternative shaped single frame on page 74. Either design can be made as a single or double frame.

As families become more mobile both nationally and internationally, sending photographs of loved ones is the next best thing to a personal visit. Quick to make and inexpensive to post, what better way is there to present the photographs which keep families in touch?

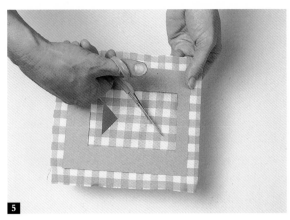

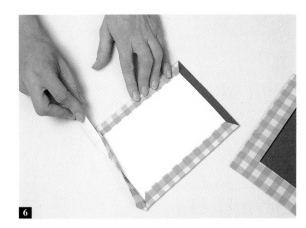

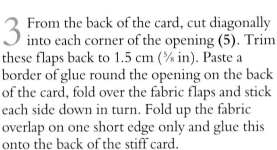

3 From the back of the card, cut diagonally into each corner of the opening (5). Trim these flaps back to 1.5 cm (⅝ in). Paste a border of glue round the opening on the back of the card, fold over the fabric flaps and stick each side down in turn. Fold up the fabric overlap on one short edge only and glue this onto the back of the stiff card.

4 Now line up this edge with the folded edge of the covered thin card, so that the right side of the paper-backed fabric covering shows through the frame window. Working from the back, paste glue to the three sides of the card, fold over the fabric flaps and press firmly into place. This leaves an opening for the photograph to be inserted. Repeat with the second frame front (6).

5 Position the two frames on the prepared backing piece with the openings at the bottom and the outer edges flush with the edges of the backing piece (7). Glue in place. Place under weights until completely dry.

The frame illustrated has been made using just one outer fabric but you could experiment with two complementary fabrics – one for the outside and one to cover the frames. Toning ribbons could be used as an inner frame as described on page 74.

61

TOOLS

1 cm (⅜ in) flat glue brush
2 cm (¾ in) flat glue brush
glue
point turner
scissors
cutting mat
steel ruler
set square
craft knife
pencil
eyelet maker and eyelets

MATERIALS

stiff card: 26 x 31 cm
 (11 x 13 in)
thin card: 35 x 40 cm
 (14 x 16 in)
outer fabric: 33 x 28 cm
 (13 x 11 in)
lining fabric: 35 x 40 cm
 (14 x 16 in)
ribbon or thick wool:
 1m (1 yd) long, 15 mm
 (½ in) wide

PREPARATION

Following the cutting plans opposite, cut out the tray shape in stiff card using the template given on the folded sheet at the back of the book and score along the dotted lines.

Cut out and label the thin card and the lining fabric pieces using the appropriate templates for the sides and adding a turning allowance of 2 cm (¾ in) all round for the fabric. Cut two of each side in both materials. The base rectangle measures 11.8 x 16.8 cm (4⅝ x 6⅝ in). Cut out and label one in thin card and one in lining fabric adding the same turning allowance.

Cufflink Tray

MAKING UP

1 Paste glue to the outside of the tray, i.e. the scored side, place centrally on the reverse of the outer fabric and press firmly. Trim the excess fabric round the shape, leaving an overlap of 1.5 cm (⅝ in).

2 Clip into each corner, right up to the stiff card, then clip each curved side with a series of "V" shapes to within 2 mm (1/12 in) of the card. Paste a border of glue to the top of each inner side, fold over the excess fabric and press firmly into place.

3 Trim each thin card lining section down to fit neatly on the sides, then cover with lining fabric. Trim the lining fabric to a 1 cm

(⅜ in) overlap on the curved sides and 2 cm (¾ in) on the long straight base side.

Clip the curved sides as for the outer fabric. Glue the clipped sides down but leave the base flaps free.

4 Glue each lining card into place but leave the base flaps free. When dry, hold the sides up at the angle you require, then glue the base flaps down onto the base of the tray.

5 Cover the thin base lining card with lining fabric. Glue in place and put under weights until dry.

6 Make one eyelet hole at each corner, thread ribbon or thick wool through and tie to hold the sides in just the right position.

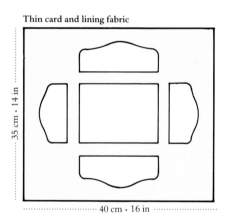

Thin card and lining fabric

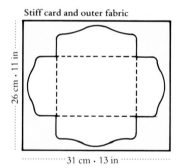

Stiff card and outer fabric

Use cufflink trays to store anything in any room. These two trays are both lined with the same delicate toile, but covered differently on the outside: one with a smart check, the other in the same toile. It is interesting to see how different these treatments look so that you can decide for yourself how your tray should be covered.

The lining is as important as the outer fabric as both are seen together, so select both carefully to complement each other and the room scheme. We used ribbon to tie one tray and thick wool for the other. Knot the wool ends tightly.

The
SITTING
ROOM

Blue and white are eternal favourites. I chose three simple fabrics to accessorize this room, mixing a simple leaf print with gingham and a shirt stripe to complement my white, hand-embroidered, linen curtains and pink walls.

I needed somewhere to store my tapestry work, my cottons and threads for mending and my knitting wools, which would be accessible and decorative, so I designed this set of boxes. They are made in the traditional manner and look wonderful stacked in a corner or in front of the window, on a side table or on a chair. The ribbon bows add a feminine touch to the striking blue and white print and also make the boxes suitable for bedroom or bathroom use. Tied ribbons are an attractive and effective closure. The gingham tray is the very simplest item to make and can be covered in anything from denim to a hand-printed silk. The prettily shaped photograph or picture frame can be made as a single or a double unit.

The basic box with attached lid is the most traditional and substantial method. Always use fabric-covered cards to line the inside to make the strongest boxes. Insert restraints in ribbon or with a small chain to protect the hinge if you wish, as shown on the cutlery box on page 89.

We glued ribbons to the outside base and lower back of these boxes and positioned them to tie at the front. You might prefer to tie them at the top for a gift box.

A pile of boxes always makes a statement in a room. Choose any number from two to five. Any more and the weight will flatten the bottom lid and it will take more time to access the contents of the lowest box.

Three Boxes

THREE BOXES (Small)

Stiff card

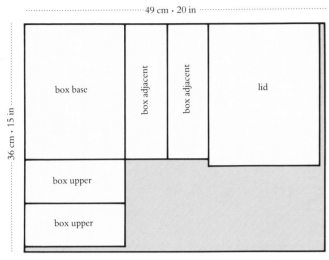

Thin card

Lining fabric

Outer fabric

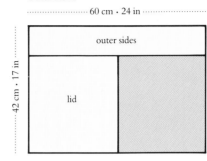

Paper-backed fabric

1 Small box

MATERIALS

stiff card: 36 x 49 cm
(15 x 20 in)
thin card: 29 x 47 cm
(12 x 19 in)
outer fabric: 42 x 60 cm
(17 x 24 in)
lining fabric: 33 x 55 cm
(13 x 22 in)
paper-backed fabric:
44 x 17 cm (18 x 7 in)
ribbon: 2 m (2 yds) long,
2.5 cm (1 in) wide
kraft paper strips

Pieces required
stiff card
adjacent sides: 22 x 7 cm
(8¾ x 2¾ in) – cut two
upper sides: 6.8 x 16.6 cm
(2⅔ x 6⁷⁄₁₂ in) – cut two
base: 22 x 16.6 cm
(8¾ x 6⁷⁄₁₂ in) – cut one
lid: 23 x 18 cm (9 x 7 in)
– cut one (to be trimmed
to size)

thin card
lid and inner base:
21.6 x 16.6 cm
(8⁷⁄₁₂ x 6½ in) – cut two
adjacent sides: 21.6 x 6.6 cm
(8⁷⁄₁₂ x 2⁷⁄₁₂ in) – cut two
upper sides: 6.6 x 16.6 cm
(2⁷⁄₁₂ x 6½ in) – cut two

outer fabric
sides: 10 x 60 cm (4 x 24 in)
– cut one
lid: 32 x 30 cm
(12½ x 12 in) – cut one

lining fabric
lid and inner base:
23.6 x 18.6 cm
(9½ x 7½ in) – cut two
adjacent sides: 23.6 x 8.6 cm
(9½ x 3½ in) – cut two
upper sides: 8.6 x 18.6 cm
(3½ x 7½ in) – cut two

paper-backed fabric
outer base: 21.8 x 16.8 cm
(8⅝ x 6⅝ in) – cut one
hinge: 21.6 x 11 cm
(8⁷⁄₁₂ x 4¼ in) – cut one

2 Medium box

THREE BOXES (Medium)

MATERIALS
stiff card: 38 x 68 cm
  (15 x 27 in)
thin card: 58 x 37 cm
  (23 x 15 in)
outer fabric: 48 x 75 cm
  (19 x 30 in)
lining fabric: 41 x 66 cm
  (17 x 27 in)
paper-backed fabric:
  58 x 21 cm (23 x 9 in)
ribbon: 2.25 m (2½ yds)
  long, 2.5 cm (1 in) wide
kraft paper strips

Pieces required
stiff card
adjacent sides: 8.7 x 29 cm
  (3⁵⁄₁₂ x 11½ in) – cut two
upper sides: 20.6 x 8.5 cm
  (8⅙ x 3⅓ in) – cut two
base: 20.6 x 29 cm
  (8⅙ x 11½ in) – cut one
lid: 31 x 22 cm
  (12 x 8¾ in) – cut one
  (to be trimmed to size)

thin card
lid and inner base:
  20.6 x 28.6 cm
  (8⅙ x 11¼ in) – cut two
adjacent sides: 8.3 x 28.6 cm
  (3¼ x 11¼ in) – cut two
upper sides: 20.6 x 8.3 cm
  (8⅙ x 3¼ in) – cut two

outer fabric
sides: 12 x 75 cm
  (4¾ x 29½ in) – cut one
lid: 36 x 34 cm
  (14½ x 13½ in) – cut one

lining fabric
lid and inner base:
  22.6 x 30.6 cm
  (9 x 12¼ in) – cut two
adjacent sides:
  10.3 x 30.6 cm
  (4¼ x 12¼ in) – cut two
upper sides: 22.6 x 10.3 cm
  (9 x 4¼ in) – cut two

paper-backed fabric
outer base: 28.8 x 20.8 cm
  (11⅜ x 8¼ in) – cut one
hinge: 28.6 x 13 cm
  (11³⁄₁₂ x 5¼ in) – cut one

Stiff card

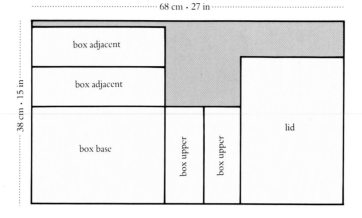

Thin card

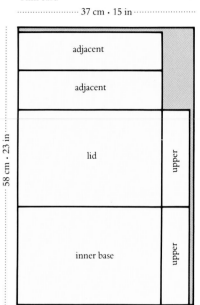

Lining fabric

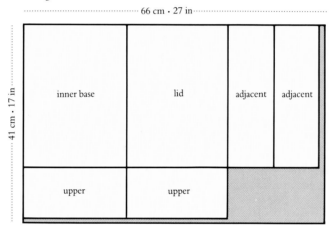

Outer fabric

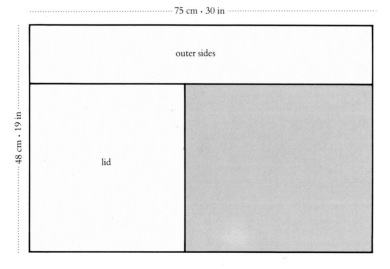

Paper-backed fabric

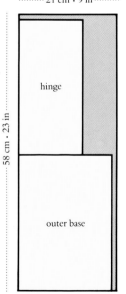

THREE BOXES (Large)

Stiff card

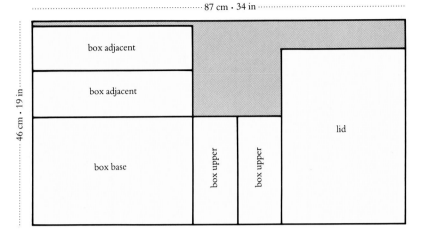

Outer fabric

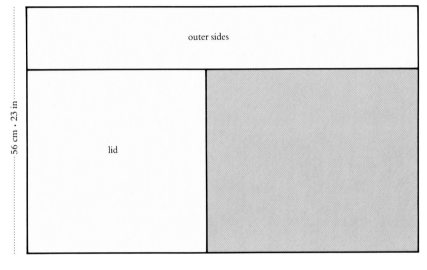

Paper-backed fabric

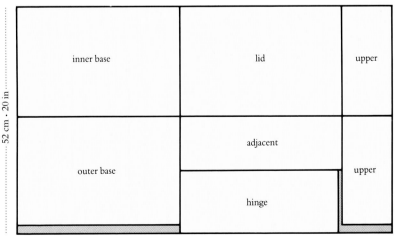

3 Large box

MATERIALS

stiff card: 46 x 87 cm
 (19 x 34 in)
outer fabric: 56 x 92 cm
 (23 x 37 in)
paper-backed fabric:
 52 x 88 cm (20 x 35 in)
ribbon: 2.50 m (2¾ yds)
 long, 2.5 cm (1 in) wide
kraft paper strips

Pieces required
stiff card
adjacent sides:
 10.5 x 37.5 cm
 (4⅙ x 14⅝ in) – cut two
upper sides: 24.6 x 10.3 cm
 (9¾ x 4¹⁄₁₂ in) – cut two
base: 24.6 x 37.5 cm
 (9¾ x 14⅝ in) – cut one
lid: 40 x 28 cm (16 x 11 in)
 – cut one (to be trimmed
 to size)

outer fabric
sides: 14 x 92 cm
 (5½ x 36¼ in) – cut one
lid: 42 x 42 cm
 (16¾ x 16¾ in) – cut one

paper-backed fabric
outer and inner base:
 25 x 38 cm (10 x 15 in)
 – cut two
adjacent side: 12 x 38 cm
 (4¾ x 15 in) – cut one
hinge: 15 x 37.1 cm
 (6 x 14⅔ in) – cut one
upper sides: 25 x 12 cm
 (10 x 4¾ in) – cut two
lid: 25 x 38 cm (10 x 15 in)
 – cut two

MAKING UP

Construct all three boxes as
described in the basic box
instructions on page 17 and
the lids following the
variation given for a hinged
lid on page 18. The small and
medium boxes are all lined
with fabric-covered card, the
large version is simply lined
with paper-backed fabric.
All have ribbon closures (see
page 66) and are lined on the
outer base with paper-backed
fabric only.

Always choose linings which are complementary to the outer fabric. Very different designs or strong contrasts are often effective, but do choose with care, bearing in mind the tenor of the whole room scheme. It is important to the creative eye that there are no shocks when the box is opened, just maybe a pleasant surprise. The lining should please you every time you open the box to use it. We all love secrets and a personal box will contain private mementoes. So choose a lining fabric which you really like rather than one which will just "do" and is purely functional. There's something special about using a fabulous fabric inside the box and a simple check, gingham or cotton on the outside.

Small Tray

MAKING UP

1 Paste glue to the outside of the tray, i.e. the scored side, place in the centre of one of the pieces of fabric and press firmly. Trim the fabric to the exact shape of the card.

2 Paste glue over the whole of the inside of the tray. Take the second piece of fabric and place this right side up in the tray. Press firmly, then trim, as before, to the exact shape of the card (1).

3 Paste a 1 cm (3/8 in) border of glue round the inner and outer top edges of the tray and cover with bias binding, folding over the end and glueing down (2).

4 Make one eyelet hole at each corner, thread ribbons through and tie to hold the sides in just the right position.

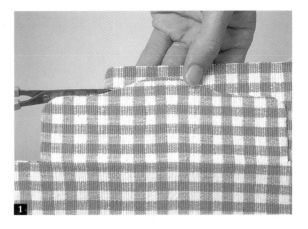

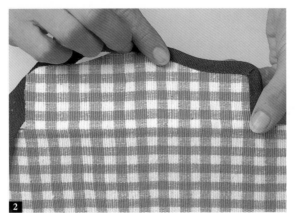

1

2

TOOLS
1 cm (3/8 in) flat glue brush
2 cm (3/4 in) flat glue brush
glue
point turner
scissors
cutting mat
steel ruler
set square
craft knife
pencil
eyelet maker and eyelets

MATERIALS
stiff card: 26 x 31 cm
 (11 x 13 in)
outer and inner fabric:
 26 x 62 cm (11 x 25 in)
bias binding: 1.10 m
 (1 1/4 yds)
ribbon: 1 m (1 yd) long,
 15 mm (1/2 in) wide

PREPARATION
Following the cutting plans on page 73, cut out the tray shape in stiff card using the template for the cufflink tray given on the folded sheet at the back of the book and score along the dotted lines. Cut the outer fabric into two pieces, each 26 x 31 cm (11 x 12 1/2 in).

To choose a lining to go with the outer fabric, put together swatches of fabric to see which work best together. Try mixing dark and light backgrounds, and utilitarian stripes with decorative floral designs.

To make this tray we
used the same template that
has been provided on the
sheet at the back of the
book for the cufflink tray
(page 63), but made it
without lining cards.

It is so very simple that
it can be completed in
minutes, using only one
piece of fabric for the
inside, one for the outside
and bias-cut tape or fabric
to bind the edges.

SINGLE PHOTOGRAPH FRAME

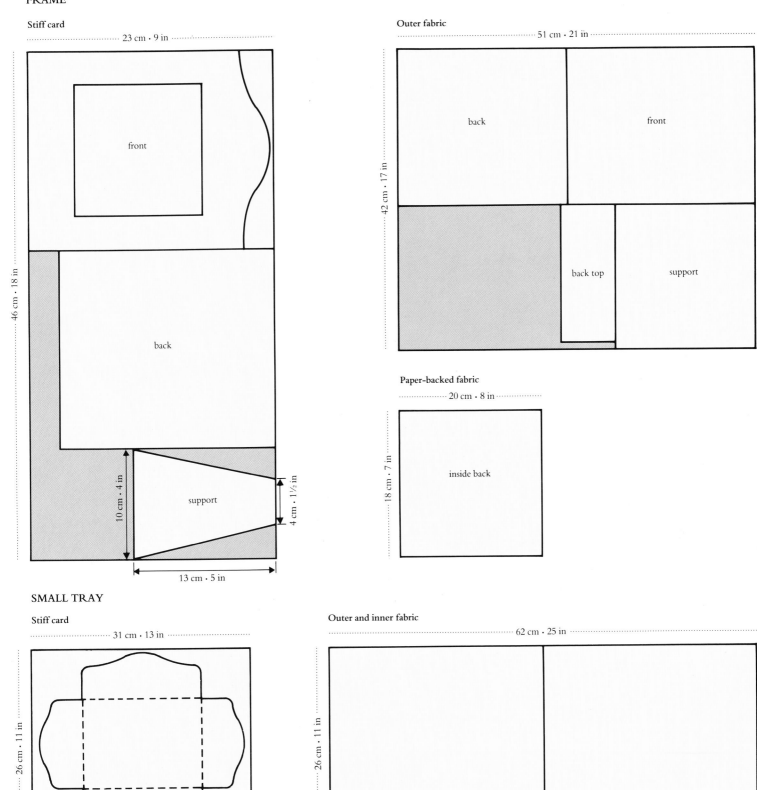

Stiff card

23 cm · 9 in

front

back

46 cm · 18 in

10 cm · 4 in

support

4 cm · 1½ in

13 cm · 5 in

Outer fabric

51 cm · 21 in

back

front

42 cm · 17 in

back top

support

Paper-backed fabric

20 cm · 8 in

inside back

18 cm · 7 in

SMALL TRAY

Stiff card

31 cm · 13 in

26 cm · 11 in

Outer and inner fabric

62 cm · 25 in

26 cm · 11 in

Single Photograph Frame

TOOLS
1 cm (⅜ in) flat glue brush
2 cm (¾ in) flat glue brush
glue
point turner
scissors
cutting mat
steel ruler
set square
craft knife
pencil

MATERIALS
stiff card: 46 x 23 cm
   (18 x 9 in)
outer fabric: 42 x 51 cm
   (17 x 21 in)
paper-backed fabric:
   18 x 20 cm (7 x 8 in)
ribbons: for support: 16 cm
   (6¼ in) long, 2.5 cm (1 in)
   wide; for frame border
   (optional): 56 cm (22 in)
   long, 2.5 cm (1 in) wide

Pieces required
stiff card
front: 18 x 23 cm (7 x 9 in)
   – cut one
back: 18 x 20 cm (7 x 8 in)
   – cut one
support: 10 x 13 cm
   (4 x 5 in) – cut one

outer fabric
front: 22 x 27 cm
   (8¾ x 10¾ in) – cut one
back: 22 x 24 cm
   (8¾ x 9½ in) – cut one
back top: 19 x 8 cm
   (7½ x 3½ in) – cut one
support: 20 x 20 cm
   (8 x 8 in) – cut one

PREPARATION
Cut out the frame front with
its central opening using the
template given on the folded
sheet at the back of the book.
Cut and label the remaining
pieces in stiff card and outer
fabric following the cutting
plans on page 73.

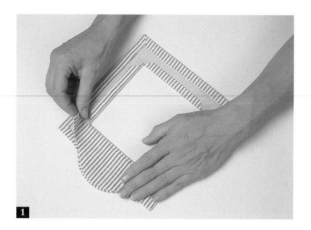

MAKING UP

1 Lay the outer fabric for the front face down on the work surface. Glue the front piece of stiff card and lay this centrally on the fabric. Make diagonal cuts in the fabric over the window, trim the flaps back to 1.5 cm (⅝ in), then fold the flaps to the back of the card and glue in place. Cut "V" shapes in the top shaped edge of the fabric, then fold the flaps over to the back and glue down.

2 Take the small piece of outer fabric for the back top and, using the covered front card as a template, lightly mark on it the shape of the frame top, so that the highest point of the curved top comes as near the top of the piece as possible. Cut along this line and glue the piece in position on the back of the frame front (1). If you wish to use ribbon to frame the opening, cut four lengths of 14 cm (5½ in) each and glue them in position on the wrong side of the opening.

3 Take the stiff card back and cover this exactly with paper-backed fabric. Glue the other side of the card and lay this centrally on the reverse of the corresponding piece of outer fabric. Trim the corners to within 5 mm (¼ in), then fold back and glue the sides down onto the paper-backed fabric (2).

4 Glue one side of the support and place on the reverse of the outer fabric, so that the

10 cm (4 in) side is 1.5 cm (⅝ in) from one edge of the fabric. Fold over the fabric overlap and glue in place. Fold in both sloping sides and trim, so that the two sides just overlap in the centre of the support. Neatly trim the overlap flush with the bottom edge of the support. On the final short side, leave an overlap of at least 3 cm (1¼ in).

Take the piece of ribbon for the support and glue 2 cm (¾ in) of one end to the bottom edge of the support.

5 To assemble the frame, paste a border of glue to both sides and the bottom of the back of the frame, leaving the top open to take the photograph. Place 2 cm (¾ in) of the other end of the ribbon centrally at the bottom, between the front and back pieces. Place under weights. When dry, line the support centrally along the bottom of the frame, then glue the fabric flap and stick in position (3).

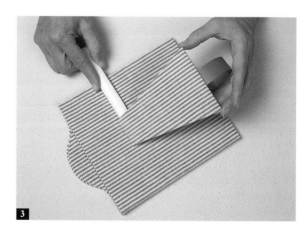

We used a blue ribbon detail as an additional frame in this pinstriped, fabric-covered frame. Smart "shirt stripes" work equally well in a chintzy room as in one with an elegant contemporary scheme, such as you might have in a study, bedroom or dining room.

Make this frame larger or smaller but remember to increase the weight of the card for a larger frame to keep the stability. We have given the template for the front on the sheet inside the back of the book - make single or double frames using the instructions given here and on page 59.

75

The
KITCHEN

I chose pretty Provençal fabrics with well-defined designs and colours for my own country kitchen. I have always loved the traditional colourings of these prints, which are more correctly called "les Indiennes". French artisans in the South copied and carved early Indian designs onto wood blocks and printed these small repetitive patterns onto calico imported from Calicut (Calcutta). Only natural dyes were used, so that although the colours – tans, ochres, blues, greens and reds – remain strong and clear, the tones are soft. Terracotta floors, old pine furniture and a traditional kitchen dresser look perfect with glazed earthenware pottery and the Provençal fabric colours.

These washable or wipe-clean cottons have deservedly found international favour and are now available worldwide.

Recipe Pad/Note Pad

TOOLS

1 cm (⅜ in) flat glue brush
2 cm (¾ in) flat glue brush
glue
point turner
scissors
cutting mat
steel ruler
set square
craft knife
pencil
sandpaper block
eyelet maker and eyelets

MATERIALS

stiff card: 21 x 28 cm
   (8¼ x 11 in)
thin card: 21 x 28 cm
   (8¼ x 11 in)
outer fabric: 48 x 17 cm
   (19 x 6¾ in)
lining fabric: 48 x 17 cm
   (19 x 6¾ in)
A5 recipe or note cards
2 articulated rings or ribbon

Pieces required

stiff card: 21 x 14 cm
   (8¼ x 5½ in) – cut two
thin card: 20.7 x 13.7 cm
   (8⅛ x 5⅜ in) – cut two
outer fabric: 24 x 17 cm
   (9½ x 6¾ in) – cut two
lining fabric: 24 x 17 cm
   (9½ x 6¾ in) – cut two

PREPARATION

Cut all the pieces of card and
fabric in half following the
measurements given above.
The lining card pieces will
need to be trimmed to obtain
the correct measurements.

Use the variation of this
method (described on
page 122) to make folders
to carry loose recipes and
other household notes.

MAKING UP

1 Use the sandpaper block to make two rounded corners on one long side of one piece of the stiff card. These two corners will be the outside edges of the pad cover. Trim the corresponding corners on the lining card to match with scissors.

2 Paste a thin layer of glue onto the outside of this piece of stiff card and cover with one of the pieces of outer fabric. Note that for the recipe pad the rounded corners are at the bottom and for the note pad these corners lie on the right hand side, so take this into account when fitting a fabric which has a directional pattern. Smooth out any air bubbles in the fabric. Trim the excess fabric to 1.5 cm (⅝ in) all round. Snip into the corners, fold over and glue the overlaps to the inside of the card.

3 Repeat with the other piece of stiff card, then treat the thin card for the lining in the same way to cover with the lining fabric. Clip away any excess fabric on the insides. Glue the lining cards to the stiff card pieces with wrong sides together and placing the lining centrally on the stiff card. Leave to dry flat under weights.

4 Make eyelets as needed, sandwich the boards round the recipe or note cards and insert rings or ribbons.

Almost unbelievably simple to make using just four pieces of card covered with fabric, for two liners and two outers, plus a bought notepad and a closure. This is an adaptation of the papers folder on page 122.

Make the notepad covers just 1 cm (³⁄₈ in) larger all round than the bought notepad. Punch holes along the top and thread together with ribbons or clip rings. Ribbons are more attractive for notepads but clip rings are extremely practical for kitchen use. Pages can be flipped over quickly and new recipe cards added with ease. We used a wipe-clean fabric for the outside and you might like to cover each finished page with cling wrap for protection.

Concertina File

TOOLS
1 cm (⅜ in) flat glue brush
2 cm (¾ in) flat glue brush
glue
point turner
scissors
cutting mat
steel ruler
set square
craft knife
pencil

MATERIALS
stiff card: 24 x 38 cm
  (10 x 15 in)
outer fabric: 30 x 45 cm
  (12 x 18 in)
paper-backed fabric:
  24 x 19 cm (10 x 8 in)
stiff paper: 64 x 58 cm
  (25 x 23 in) - makes 4
  inserts
ribbon: 50 cm (½ yd) long,
  15 mm (½ in) wide

Pieces required
stiff card
sides: 23.5 x 17 cm
  (9¼ x 6¾ in) - cut two
spine: 23.5 x 3.5 cm
  (9¼ x 1½ in) - cut one

paper-backed fabric
inner spine: 23.5 x 10 cm
  (9¼ x 4 in) - cut one
corners: 17 x 8.5 cm
  (7 x 3½ in) - cut into four
  triangles

PREPARATION
Cut out and label all the
pieces in card and paper-
backed fabric following the
cutting plans on page 82.
   Cut out as many concertina inserts as required from
stiff paper following the
cutting plan on page 82, then
mark the score lines (i.e. the
dotted lines).

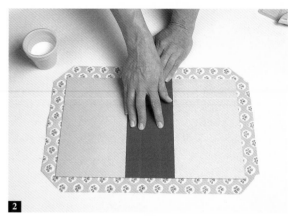

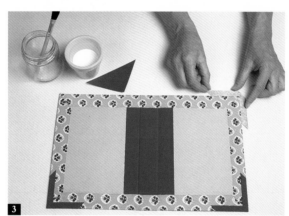

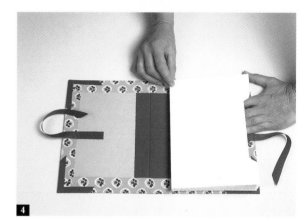

MAKING UP

1 Make up the concertina inserts by folding and glueing each of the individual sheets following the scored lines (1). Leave to dry, then glue the pockets together, taking care not to glue the very bottom strip of each one to the next. Insert a piece of stiff card about 20 x 15 cm (8 x 6 in) into each and leave under weights to dry.

2 Place the outer fabric right side down. Glue the cards for the sides and spine and position centrally on the fabric with a 4 mm (⅙ in) gap between the pieces. Trim the fabric corners to within 5 mm (¼ in) of the card.

3 Take the inner spine fabric and glue this centrally, so that it covers the centre card and extends an equal amount onto each side card. Press well (2). Fold in the sides and glue down, then fold in the top and bottom and glue down.

4 To make the contrast corners, place one of the paper-backed fabric corner pieces face down on the work surface and position one of the file corners right side down on top, leaving a 1.5 cm (⅝ in) overlap on both sides. Mark and glue the corners as described on page 28, then glue down the corner flaps (3). Repeat for the other three corners.

5 Cut the ribbon in half and position each one approximately 5 cm (2 in) from the edge in the centre of each side. Glue in place and leave flat under weights to dry. When completely dry, paste glue to one side of the concertina insert and position on the corre-sponding side of the file (4). Leave this under weights until completely dry before repeating the process for the other side.

This file is used in my kitchen as a portable letter rack, to hold business cards, correspondence, household bills, postcards and lists. I rather like the strong contrast provided by the red corners and ties against the sunflower yellow of the main fabrics. Dark green or blue would have been equally effective with this fabric whereas a plain yellow would have shown an obvious corner but no interesting contrast.

The inside pieces are straightforward to make following the cutting and scoring lines shown on the next page. Make up to eight inserts for this size of file, depending on the use.

CONCERTINA FILE

Stiff card

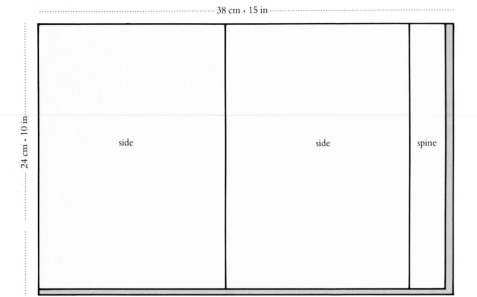

Paper-backed fabric

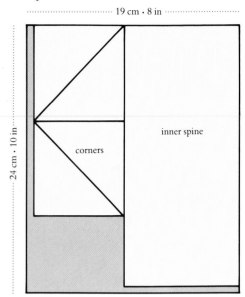

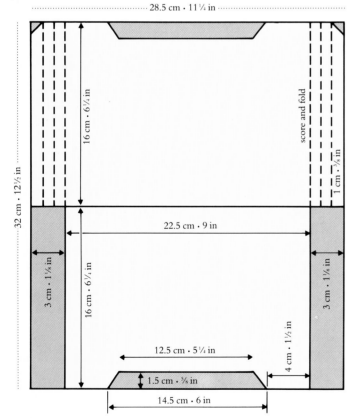

Stiff paper

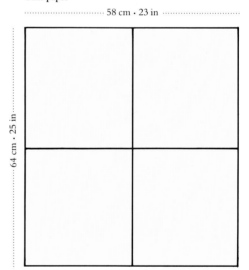

Pencil Pot

MAKING UP

1 Cut four strips of kraft paper, each 8 cm (3⅛ in) long and 3 cm (1¼ in) wide. Fold in half lengthways, matt side to the middle.

2 Paste a 1.5 cm (⅝ in) border of glue onto one side of the base, open out a strip of kraft paper and slip it onto the pot base, so that one half is glued and the other half forms a free flap. Repeat to glue the other three pieces onto the other three sides of the base. This will produce a base with four free flaps of kraft paper.

3 Place the base, so that the glued strips are underneath. Take one of the adjacent side pieces, paste a thin border of glue to the base of the card and position against one side of the base, with the glued side facing out. Bring up the kraft paper flap into position and stick to the side piece. Repeat with the other adjacent side piece.

4 Take one of the upper sides, paste glue to each thin side edge and in a thin border across the bottom, then slide in between the two adjacent sides. Bring up the kraft paper flap and stick to the side piece. Repeat with the remaining upper side piece.

5 Next cut lengths of kraft paper 10 cm (4 in) long and 3 cm (1¼ in) wide and fold in half. Paste glue in a thin border on both sides of each corner of the pot, slide over the kraft paper strips and press in place to strengthen each corner.

6 This will make a firm box, but if you wish to strengthen the box further, strips of kraft paper may be applied in the same way to all inside joins of the box. Use the sandpaper block to make sure that the top edges are all level (1).

7 Press the fabric to remove any creases. Starting at one corner of the box, paste a

1

1 cm (⅜ in) border of glue down one side and position one short end of the fabric over this border, keeping an equal overlap of fabric at both top and bottom.

8 Keeping the fabric taut and the pattern running along the top line, glue each side in turn and press the fabric into place. Neaten the final corner with a fold under if the fabric is thin enough and an accurately cut edge if the fabric is too thick to make a neat fold.

At each top corner remove the excess fabric as described on page 18 (step 3). Glue the resulting four flaps down inside the box. Use the turner to give a neat finish to the corners. Cut the corners at the base and glue down in the same way.

9 Cut the paper-backed fabric into four side pieces and two bases as follows: two side pieces 11 x 8 cm (4¼ x 3¼ in), two side pieces 11 x 7.5 cm (4¼ x 3 in), inner base 7.5 x 8 cm (3 x 3¼ in) and outer base 9.5 x 9 cm (3¾ x 3½ in).

Checking each piece against the relevant side and trimming where necessary, paste one inside side of the pot and place the paper-backed fabric over. Position the piece so that it sits 2 mm (1/12 in) below the top edge and runs onto the base. Use the turner to make a crisp edge at the inside base of the pot. Finger press to secure.

Repeat with the other sides, then fit the inner and outer bases.

TOOLS
1 cm (⅜ in) flat glue brush
2 cm (¾ in) flat glue brush
glue
point turner
scissors
cutting mat
steel ruler
set square
craft knife
pencil
sandpaper block

MATERIALS
stiff card: 16 x 28 cm
  (7 x 12 in)
outer fabric: 13 x 36 cm
  (6 x 15 in)
paper-backed fabric:
  11 x 46 cm (5 x 19 in)
kraft paper

Pieces required
stiff card
adjacent sides: 8 x 10 cm
  (3¼ x 4 in) – cut two
upper sides: 8 x 9.8 cm
  (3¼ x 3¹¹/₁₂ in) – cut two
base: 8 x 8 cm (3¼ x 3¼ in)
  – cut one

paper-backed fabric
adjacent sides: 11 x 8 cm
  (4¼ x 3¼ in) – cut two
upper sides: 11 x 7.5 cm
  (4¼ x 3 in) – cut two
bases: 8 x 7.5 cm
  (3¼ x 3 in) – cut two

PREPARATION
Cut out and label all the pieces in card, outer and paper-backed fabric following the cutting plans on page 85.

PENCIL POT

Stiff card

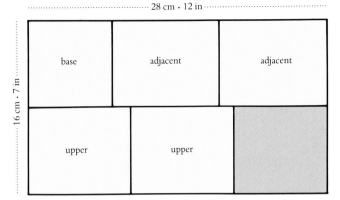

Paper-backed fabric

KITCHEN TRAY

Outer and lining fabric

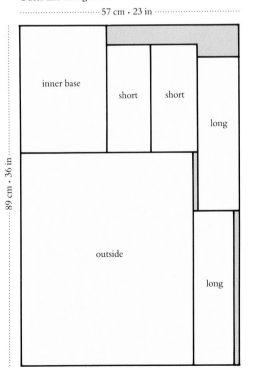

Stiff and thin card

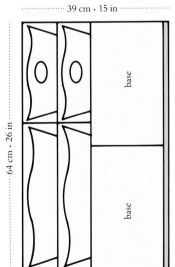

There is not a room in the house where a simple pencil pot would not be useful. Make this pot for pens and pencils, make-up brushes, scissors and small house-hold tools, cotton wool, small kitchen utensils or a larger version for kitchen tools, sewing threads or cutlery.

We added a double base to the basic measurements and method described on page 83. To do this, cut two extra pieces in stiff card, one 1 cm ($\frac{3}{8}$ in) and one 2 cm ($\frac{3}{4}$ in) larger all round than the finished pot. Cover each with fabric. Glue together, then glue to the bottom of the pencil pot. Insert a weight and leave to dry overnight until the base is securely fixed.

Trays which are both decorative and functional are difficult to find and one which also works with your colour scheme is almost impossible, so make your own fabric-covered trays using small prints, checks, florals or stripes. Try to find a wipe-clean fabric which is not too thick to make a neat overlap at the corners.

This tray with its double thickness of base is extremely strong and is designed to hold the breakfast jars or a coffee pot, milk jug and cups and saucers for four.

Kitchen Tray

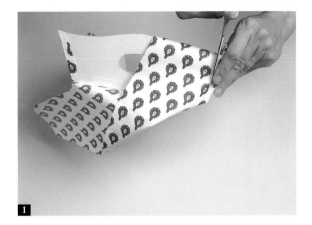

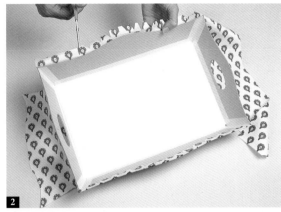

TOOLS
1 cm (⅜ in) flat glue brush
2 cm (¾ in) flat glue brush
glue
point turner
scissors
cutting mat
steel ruler
set square
craft knife
pencil

MATERIALS
stiff card: 64 x 39 cm
  (26 x 15 in)
thin card: 64 x 39 cm
  (26 x 15 in)
outer and lining fabric:
  89 x 57 cm (36 x 23 in)
kraft paper strips

Pieces required
stiff card
long sides: 38 x 9 cm
  (15 x 3½ in) – cut two
short sides: 26 x 9 cm
  (10¼ x 3½ in) – cut two
bases: 32 x 20.1 cm
  (12⁷⁄₁₂ x 7¹¹⁄₁₂ in) – cut two

thin card
long sides: 38 x 9 cm
  (15 x 3½ in) – cut two
short sides: 26 x 9 cm
  (10¼ x 3½ in) – cut two
bases: 32 x 20.1 cm
  (12⁷⁄₁₂ x 7¹¹⁄₁₂ in) – cut two

outer and lining fabric
outside: 55 x 45 cm
  (22 x 18 in) – cut one
long sides: 40 x 12 cm
  (16 x 5 in) – cut two
short sides: 28 x 12 cm
  (11 x 5 in) – cut two
inner base: 34 x 22 cm
  (14 x 9 in) – cut one

PREPARATION
Cut out and label the sides in
stiff and thin card using the
templates given on the folded
sheet at the back of the book.
Cut out and label two base
pieces in stiff card and one in
thin card. Cut the handle
holes in the two short sides of
the stiff card.

Cut out and label the outer
and lining fabric following
the cutting plan on page 85.

MAKING UP

1 Glue the two base pieces together for a firmer construction. Kraft paper flaps onto the base as described on page 17.

Glue one long side at an angle, then the second (adjoining) side, so that the sides meet and abut. Kraft the angle, inside and out. Continue with side three and finally side four. Check that all angles inside and out are kraft-ed.

2 Paste glue over the outer base of the tray and place centrally on the reverse of the outer fabric. Glue the two long sides and pull the fabric up against the sides; press firmly.

3 Trim the overlap at the corners, so that there is a 1 cm (⅜ in) overlap at each corner which folds onto the short side. Stick this flap down and trim the excess fabric on the long sides to 2 cm (¾ in), following the shape of the side (1).

Clip along the length to within 3 mm (⅛ in) of the card. Trim away the excess fabric at the corners and glue the fabric down to the inside of the tray sides (2).

4 On a flat surface, tip the box onto its short side with the fabric underneath. With a pencil, lightly mark the length of both corners on the reverse of the fabric (3). Cut along these lines in order to trim the fabric to the exact size of the short side. Glue in place,

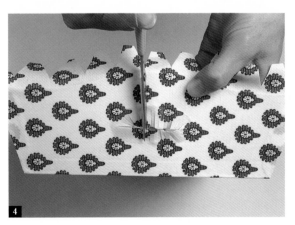

trim the top edge to 2 cm (¾ in), clip and glue down to the inside.

5 Carefully slash the fabric across the middle of the handle opening, then make small cuts to within 2 mm (¹⁄₁₂ in) of the card all round (4). Glue the resulting fabric flaps to the inside. Repeat for the second short side.

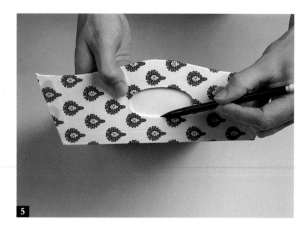

6 Trim all three straight edges on the sides and base of the lining cards until they fit their respective sides inside the tray when placed 2 mm (1/12 in) below the top edge.

7 Position the first short side in the tray and from the outside draw the handle opening in pencil on the card (5).
   Remove the card, then enlarge this opening by 1 mm (1/16 in) all round and cut out the centre (6).

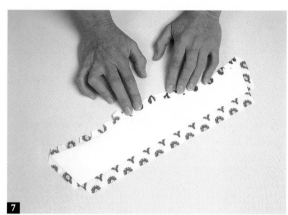

8 Cover in lining fabric and cut out the handle hole as for the outer fabric (step 5). Clip the top curved edge and glue down, leaving both side flaps and bottom flap free. Trim the corners. Paste glue to the short side, including a 1 cm (3/8 in) strip onto the base and onto each adjoining side. Glue the card in place. (As this is the first card to be glued into place, both side flaps are left free. The next card to be glued in will have one side folded over and the other free.)
   Cover the remaining three lining sides (7), cutting the handle hole in the second short side as before. Glue the lining cards into position in the tray in sequence following the technique given on page 24.
   Measure the internal base, cut out in thin card, cover and glue in place.

Cutlery boxes need not only be for the best cutlery. Use strong outer and lining fabrics which will stand up to continuous usage and be easy to maintain.

I chose the sunflower yellow with French navy and white to sit on my pine dresser among the terra-cotta and country crockery to hold my blue handled kitchen cutlery. Dark blue

liners take the heat off the strong colours but are given interest with the outer fabric detail at the top of the divisions. Fabric-covered lining cards will make the strongest box but paper-backed fabric or felt will be quicker and will be strong enough provided 3mm (⅛ in) card is used for the dividers. I have used a combination of the outer

fabric and paper-backed fabric to line this box.

Follow the instructions on pages 17 and 18 for the basic box with hinged lid and make divisions to suit your requirements following the instructions on page 30.

I chose three dividers for this box making four sections to take my day-to-day kitchen cutlery.

TOOLS

1 cm ($\frac{3}{8}$ in) flat glue brush
2 cm ($\frac{3}{4}$ in) flat glue brush
glue
point turner
scissors
cutting mat
steel ruler
set square
craft knife
pencil

MATERIALS

stiff card: 42 x 108 cm
   (17 x 43 in)
thin card: 81 x 31 cm
   (32 x 13 in)
outer fabric: 50 x 100 cm
   (20 x 40 in)
paper-backed fabric:
   67 x 96 cm (27 x 38 in)
wadding: 40 x 28 cm
   (16 x 11 in)
ribbon: 40 cm (16 in) long,
   7 mm ($\frac{1}{4}$ in) wide
kraft paper strips

Pieces required
stiff card
adjacent sides: 7 x 40 cm
   ($2\frac{3}{4}$ x $15\frac{3}{4}$ in) – cut two
upper sides: 6.8 x 27.6 cm
   ($2\frac{2}{3}$ x $10\frac{5}{6}$ in) – cut two
base: 27.6 x 40 cm
   ($10\frac{5}{6}$ x $15\frac{3}{4}$ in) – cut one
lid: 28.2 x 40.4 cm
   ($11\frac{1}{6}$ x 16 in) – cut one
divisions: 6.8 x 27.6 cm
   ($2\frac{2}{3}$ x $10\frac{5}{6}$ in) – cut three

thin card
lid: 40.4 x 30.2 cm
   (16 x 12 in) – cut one
lid lining: 40.4 x 28.2 cm
   (16 x $11\frac{1}{6}$ in) – cut one

outer fabric
sides: 10 x 100 cm
   (4 x 40 in) – cut one
division tops: 2 x 27.6 cm
   ($\frac{3}{4}$ x 11 in) – cut three
lid: 40 x 45 cm
   ($15\frac{3}{4}$ x $17\frac{3}{4}$ in) – cut one

Continued on page 91

CUTLERY BOX

Stiff card

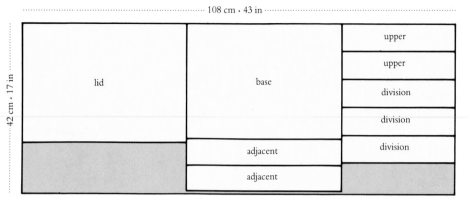

Outer fabric

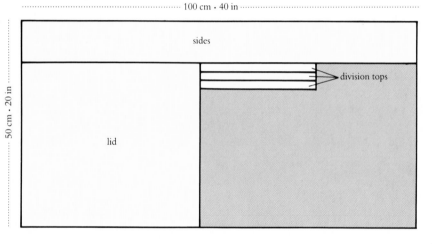

Paper-backed fabric

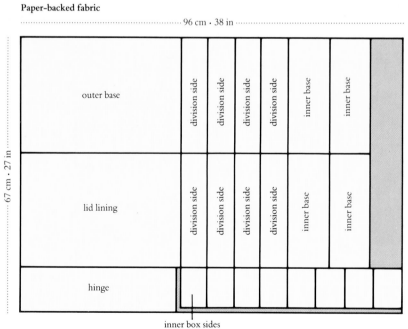

Thin card

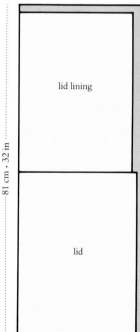

Cutlery Box

MAKING UP

1 Mark in pencil on the stiff card base of the box where the divisions are to go.

2 Construct the box following the basic instructions on page 17 and the variation for the hinged lid on page 18 up to the point where the internal hinge is glued in position. Remember to check that the pencil marked side of the base is on the inside of the box.

3 To make the divisions, glue the top of each card division and cover with the narrow strips of outer fabric, ensuring that the fabric is the exact length of the cards (1).

Kraft the divisions in place (see page 30) along the base, on each side of the division and in the corners made by the card against the back and front of the box. Be careful, however, to make these pieces of kraft paper at least 5 mm (¼ in) shorter than the division height otherwise they will show above the lining fabric.

4 Working on each of the four sections in turn, line the sides and bases with the paper-backed fabric. Remember at this stage to glue in the ribbons that will form the hinge restraints. Glue these to the box sides before adding the lining at approximately 6 cm (2½ in) from the back of the box and angled at 45° towards the back.

5 Continue with the hinged lid construction as described on page 18 and fix in position. Cover the lid lining card and before glueing, fix the other ends of the ribbon hinge restraints onto the lid, so that they are long enough to hold the lid at an angle just past the vertical.

Glue in the lid lining and cover the outer base of the box with paper-backed fabric (2).

Continued from page 90

paper-backed fabric
lid and outer base: 28 x 40 cm
(11 x 15¾ in) – cut two
hinge: 11 x 39.6 cm
(4½ x 15⁷⁄₁₂ in) – cut one
division sides: 7 x 28 cm
(2¾ x 11 in) – cut eight
inner bases: 28 x 10 cm
(11 x 4 in) – cut four
inner box sides: 10 x 7 cm
(4 x 2¾ in) – cut eight

PREPARATION

Cut out and label all the pieces in stiff and thin card, outer and paper-backed fabric following the cutting plans on page 90.

Cut the ribbon in half to make two hinge restraints.

The
DESK

The home desk has become more and more difficult to keep organized with the increase in household accounts, personal correspondence, insurance forms, subscriptions, etc, which we all have to deal with. We also need to keep track of the important dates for friends and families - anniversaries, birthdays and so on. Although there are many and varied files and folders available to purchase, your own fabric-covered system will be much more attractive, versatile and can be made to fit your needs and your design scheme exactly. We have designed folders, boxes, files and trays to accommodate the particular problems of keeping household paperwork in order.

Our tightly woven, printed cotton in deep colours was chosen to show as little dirt as possible even with extensive use and the lovely fresh floral design was added to complement the main fabric as an interesting contrast.

An attractive and functional present for a male friend. Of course it is equally suitable for a female friend but most of us have more problems finding presents for men than for women. Almost any tightly woven fabric can be used, but adjust the spine measurements for a very heavy fabric. Experiment with ties, tassels and knots for a decorative closure. Use two different fabrics inside and out or make contrast corners for a change.

Blotter

MAKING UP

1 Lay the outer fabric right side down on a flat surface. Glue the large piece of card and lay centrally onto the fabric. Paste glue to the two 1.5 cm (⅝ in) strips and place these one on either side of the card. Glue each of the side cards and place these next to the card strips. Press well, turn over and press again.

2 Trim the excess fabric at the corners to within 2 mm (¹⁄₁₂ in) of each corner. Fold over the sides and glue in place, then fold over the top and bottom and glue down.
   Take the two pieces of inner spine fabric and glue one over each strip of card (1).

3 Cover the two side lining cards with the contrast fabric and glue in place.

4 Cover the blotter card with the outer fabric. Take the four corner pieces and cover with contrast fabric. Trim the excess fabric at the corners to within 5 mm (¼ in) of the corner, fold over the long side and glue down, leaving the other two fabric flaps free. Repeat for the other three corners.
   Position the corners on the covered blotter card so that the right side of the blotter card is against the wrong side of the corner piece (2). Glue the two flaps down. Repeat for all four corners, then glue this whole card into place (3). Place under weights until completely dry.
   Insert the blotting paper, trimming to fit if necessary and fold over the sides.

TOOLS

1 cm (⅜ in) flat glue brush
2 cm (¾ in) flat glue brush
glue
point turner
scissors
cutting mat
steel ruler
set square
craft knife
pencil

MATERIALS

stiff card: 35 x 56 cm
   (14 x 22 in)
thin card: 35 x 62 cm
   (14 x 25 in)
outer fabric: 42 x 109 cm
   (17 x 43 in)
contrast fabric: 38 x 44 cm
   (15 x 18 in)
blotting paper: 28 x 35 cm
   (11 x 14 in)

Pieces required
stiff card
sides: 35 x 14 cm
   (13¾ x 5½ in) – cut two
main blotter: 35 x 28 cm
   (13¾ x 11 in) – cut one

thin card
sides: 34.6 x 13.6 cm
   (13⁷⁄₁₂ x 5⅓ in) – cut two
strips: 35 x 1.5 cm
   (13¾ x ⅝ in) – cut two
main blotter: 34.6 x 27.6 cm
   (13⁷⁄₁₂ x 10⅗ in) – cut one
corners: 8 x 4 cm
   (4 x 2 in) – cut one

outer fabric
back: 42 x 67 cm
   (16½ x 26½ in) – cut one
inner spines: 34.6 x 6 cm
   (13¾ x 2½ in) – cut two
blotter cover: 37 x 30 cm
   (14½ x 12 in) – cut one

contrast fabric
sides: 38 x 17 cm
   (15 x 6¾ in) – cut two
corners: 20 x 10 cm
   (8 x 4 in) – cut one

PREPARATION

Cut out and label all the pieces in stiff and thin card, outer and contrast fabric following the cutting plans on page 98.

Concertina File

The size and method of making up this concertina file are exactly the same as the kitchen file on page 80.

Make with as many inserts as you wish - a maximum of ten can be accommodated with this width of spine - and use to keep correspondence, accounts, cards or stationery in order.

96

Boxes

A selection of boxes, all with separate lids, to show some of the many different permutations which can be achieved following the formulae and basic methods given on pages 16 to 22.

These boxes are specially sized to take standard business and home letters and papers. Organize your desk at home or at work by using these boxes to store unused stationery, letters and accounts. Make the boxes deeper if desired but sometimes fewer papers in more boxes are easier to organize than more papers in fewer boxes.

BLOTTER

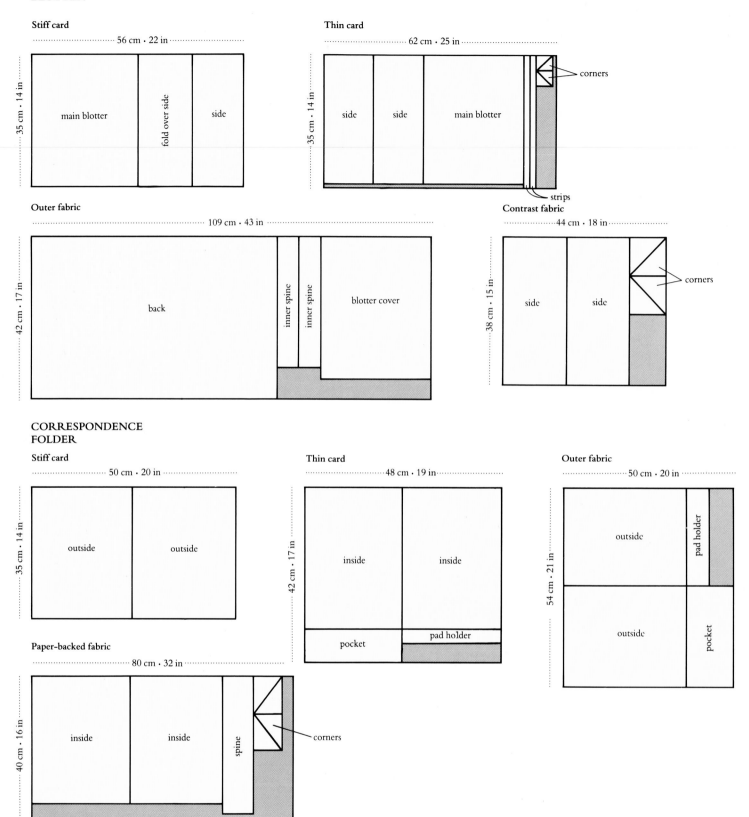

Stiff card

56 cm · 22 in

35 cm · 14 in

main blotter | fold over side | side

Thin card

62 cm · 25 in

35 cm · 14 in

side | side | main blotter

corners

strips

Outer fabric

109 cm · 43 in

42 cm · 17 in

back | inner spine | inner spine | blotter cover

Contrast fabric

44 cm · 18 in

38 cm · 15 in

side | side

corners

CORRESPONDENCE FOLDER

Stiff card

50 cm · 20 in

35 cm · 14 in

outside | outside

Thin card

48 cm · 19 in

42 cm · 17 in

inside | inside

pocket | pad holder

Outer fabric

50 cm · 20 in

54 cm · 21 in

outside | pad holder

outside | pocket

Paper-backed fabric

80 cm · 32 in

40 cm · 16 in

inside | inside | spine

corners

Correspondence Folder

MAKING UP

1 Paste glue in a thin layer on one side of one of the pieces of stiff card. Place one of the outer fabric pieces right side down and position the card carefully onto the fabric, glued side down, so that one long side of the card lies flush with one long side of the fabric, leaving a 2 cm (¾ in) overlap on the other three sides.

Turn over and press the fabric firmly onto the card, smoothing out any bubbles.

2 Trim the excess fabric at the two outside corners across at an angle, to within 5 mm (¼ in) of the card. Fold over and glue down the fabric overlaps (1).

Repeat with the other corner. This makes one side of the folder. Make up the other side in the same way.

3 To make up the inside pieces of the folder, use the two pieces of thin card and the two pieces of paper-backed fabric. Glue the card as before, then position centrally over the fabric with equal overlaps on all four sides. Cut all four corners to within 2 mm (¹/₁₂ in) of the card, then fold and neaten as above. Place under weights to dry.

4 To make the contrast corners, cut the 20 x 10 cm (8 x 4 in) piece of paper-backed fabric into four triangles. Place one of the corner pieces right side down on the work

surface. Position one of the outside folder edges (not the raw-edged corners) over this piece, leaving a 1.5 cm (⅝ in) overlap on both sides. Pencil around the corner, thus marking the exact area to be glued (2).

Carefully paste glue within the pencilled triangle, reposition the corner of the folder along these lines and press firmly. Cut across the excess fabric at the corner to within 5 mm (¼ in) of the card. Glue the corner flaps, folding over each one in turn, press firmly and neaten with the point turner. Repeat with the other three outside corners.

5 Cut the piece of paper-backed fabric for the spine into two pieces, one 9.5 x 39 cm (3¾ x 15⅓ in) and the other 6.5 x 34 cm (2¾ x 13½ in). The wider piece will be the outer spine and the narrower piece the inner. Place the outer spine right side down on the work surface and mark two lines along the length,

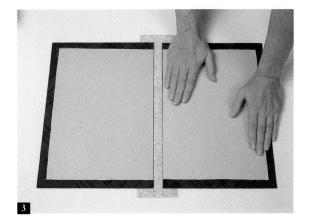

TOOLS
1 cm (⅜ in) flat glue brush
2 cm (¾ in) flat glue brush
glue
point turner
scissors
cutting mat
steel ruler
set square
craft knife
pencil

MATERIALS
stiff card: 35 x 50 cm
  (14 x 20 in)
thin card: 42 x 48 cm
  (17 x 19 in)
outer fabric: 54 x 50 cm
  (21 x 20 in)
paper-backed fabric:
  40 x 80 cm (16 x 32 in)
ribbon: 50 cm (20 in) long,
  15 mm (½ in) wide

Pieces required
stiff card
outsides: 35 x 25 cm
  (13¾ x 9¾ in) - cut two

thin card
insides: 34 x 24 cm
  (13¼ x 9¼ in) - cut two
pocket: 8 x 24 cm
  (3¼ x 9¼ in) - cut one
pad holder: 2 x 24 cm
  (¾ x 9¼ in) - cut one

outer fabric
outsides: 27 x 39 cm
  (10½ x 15⅓ in) - cut two
pocket: 27 x 11 cm
  (10½ x 4½ in) - cut one
pad holder: 27 x 4 cm
  (10½ x 1½ in) - cut one

paper-backed fabric
insides: 37 x 27 cm
  (14½ x 10½) - cut two
spine: 39 x 16 cm
  (15¼ x 6½ in) - cut one
corners: 20 x 10 cm
  (8 x 4 in) - cut one

PREPARATION
Cut out and label all the pieces in stiff and thin card, outer and paper-backed fabric following the cutting plans on page 98.

4

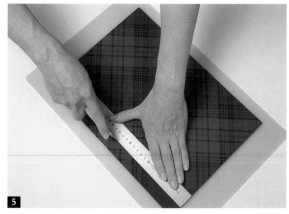

5

3.5 cm (1⅓ in) in from each side and a line across the width 2 cm (¾ in) down from the top. Paste glue onto to one of the 3.5 cm (1⅓ in) marked strips. Place one of the outside folder pieces, right side down, onto the spine piece, positioning the long raw edge without the corners against the marked line.

Turn over and press firmly. Repeat with the other folder side, checking that the sides line up accurately with the pencilled lines **(3)**. Glue the flaps at the top and bottom, fold to the inside and press firmly. Glue the inside spine and position over the joins. Place under weights to dry.

Do not be tempted to bend the folder at this stage or the spine will be weakened.

6 To make the pocket, take the relevant piece of thin card and the corresponding piece of outer fabric. Apply glue to one side of the card and stick this centrally to the wrong side of the fabric. Glue down the top flap and cut across the bottom corners this time to within 1 cm (⅜ in) of the card.

7 Now take one of the inner cards and position the pocket at the bottom, with the right side of the inner card to the wrong side of the pocket. Working from the wrong side, you will now have three flaps, one on each side and one on the bottom. Glue these three flaps onto the back of the inner card **(4)**.

If you wish, you can insert a piece of thick-ish card between the inner card and the pocket before you glue it. This will give the pocket slightly more volume but be careful not to pull so tightly that the card cannot be removed once the flaps have dried.

8 To make the writing pad holder, take the relevant strip of thin card and glue this centrally onto the wrong side of the remaining outer fabric strip. Fold over the top and the bottom and glue.

Position on the right side of the second inner card 3-4 cm (1- 1½ in) from the top. Glue the flaps in place on the back, leaving enough room to slip a piece of card behind.

9 To make the ties, working from the front of the folder, measure 2.5 cm (1 in) in from the outside edges and halfway down the lengths. Using a craft knife, cut slits in the card to the exact width of the ribbon **(5)**. Ease the ribbon through from front to back with the help of the knife point, taking care not to stretch the slit. Pull 2 cm (¾ in) through and glue to the inside of the card to secure.

10 Spread glue to the inside of the covered inner pieces. Place carefully into position on the inside of the folder and press in place **(6)**. Leave flat under weights until completely dry.

6

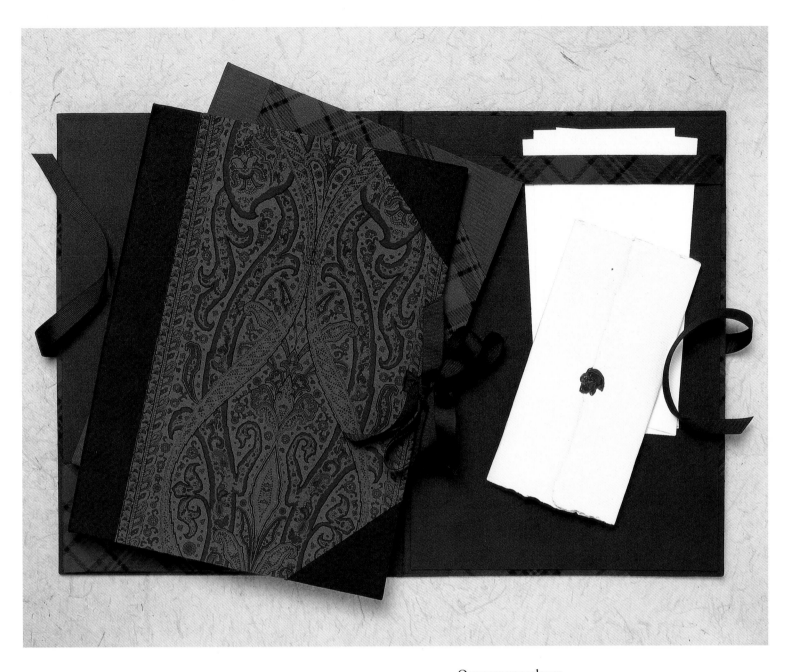

Our correspondence folder is designed to be simple but smart, for home or business use. Choose a fabric which will not show the dirt easily and always add protective corners in paper-backed fabric or leather. Paisleys and checks look particularly good but so, too, do stripes. You could also experiment with hand-marbled papers for an alternative finish.

Desk Tray

TOOLS

1 cm (⅜ in) flat glue brush
2 cm (¾ in) flat glue brush
glue
point turner
scissors
cutting mat
steel ruler
set square
craft knife
pencil
eyelet maker and eyelets

MATERIALS

stiff card: 30 x 36 cm
   (12 x 15 in)
thin card: 45 x 50 cm
   (18 x 20 in)
outer fabric: 32 x 38 cm
   (13 x 15 in)
lining fabric: 45 x 50 cm
   (18 x 20 in)
ribbon: 2.25 m (2¼ yds)
   long, 7 mm (¼ in) wide

PREPARATION

Following the cutting plans
below, cut out the tray
shape in stiff card using the
template given on the folded
sheet at the back of the book
and score along the dotted
lines.

   Cut out and label the thin
card and the lining fabric
pieces using the appropriate
templates for the sides and
adding a turning allowance of
2 cm (¾ in) all round for the
fabric. The base rectangle
measures 15.8 x 21.8 cm
(6¼ x 8½ in). Cut out and
label one in card and one in
lining fabric adding the same
turning allowance.

MAKING UP

1 Paste glue to the outside of the tray, i.e. the scored side, place centrally on the reverse of the outer fabric and press firmly. Trim the excess fabric round the shape, leaving an overlap of 1.5 cm (⅝ in).

2 Clip into each corner, right up to the stiff card, then clip each curved side with a series of "V" shapes to within 2 mm (¹⁄₁₂ in) of the card. Paste a border of glue to the top of each inner side, fold over the excess fabric and press firmly into place.

3 Trim each thin card lining section down to fit neatly on the sides, then cover with lining fabric. Trim the lining fabric to a 1 cm (⅜ in) overlap on the curved sides and 2 cm (¾ in) on the long straight base side.
   Clip the curved side and glue the clipped sides down but leave the base flaps free.

4 Glue each lining card into place but leave the base flaps free (1). When dry, hold the sides up at the required angle, then glue the base flaps onto the base of the tray.

5 Cover the thin base card with lining fabric. Glue in place and put under weights until dry (2).

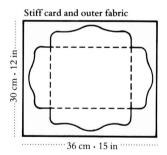

6 Make two eyelet holes at each corner, thread ribbons through and tie (3).

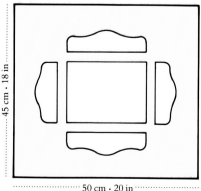

Stiff card and outer fabric

30 cm · 12 in

36 cm · 15 in

Thin card and lining fabric

45 cm · 18 in

50 cm · 20 in

A functional and extremely
decorative accessory for use
in any room but especially
to control desk clutter,
such as pens, papers and
general small office equipment. Cover inner and
outer cards with the same
fabric or mix checks and
plains, stripes and florals,
always keeping the colour
tones the same and suiting
the fabric to the purpose.

Desk Tray Variation

We used the simplest cotton gingham to show how even the most ordinary fabric which we are so used to seeing and taking for granted can be given a new lease of life on cartonnage pieces.

These decorative trays are all made to the same shape, size and method as the cufflink trays on page 63. We have filled them with a varied range of objects as a small sample of the huge potential for storage that these simple but elegant pieces possess.

Pencil Pot

Another simple remedy for tidying up desk equipment. This pencil pot is one of the simplest pieces of cartonnage to make, as described on page 83.

The
BATHROOM

One of the main secrets of soft furnishings in interior design is to use good fabrics well and with imagination. Fabrics should not be over used and strong designs should only be used sparingly. For my bathroom I had selected a linen, hand-printed with a variety of marvellous decoy ducks, but felt that the design as a whole would be too overpowering for a small room. The solution was to buy enough fabric to include my favourite ducks and to appliqué them to a smart but less dominant stripe before making up the boxes and storage bins which I had designed.

I carried on the theme by using the larger ducks from the same design to appliqué onto tea towelling which I then made into guest hand towels.

Ideal for storing hand towels and flannels in the bathroom, this bin may be made using the template provided on the sheet inside the back cover.

I selected three ducks from a furnishing fabric design to fit the front of the bin and stitched them in position as described on page 112.

Make the same bin for other rooms of the house to take waste paper or to store magazines or children's toys, again with appropriate motifs appliquéd or stencilled to one or more of the sides.

Storage Bin

MAKING UP

1 If using an applied motif, cut it out and pin it at 1 cm (⅜ in) intervals centrally to one of the outer fabric sides. Machine in position using a satin stitch or hand sew with a blanket stitch. Remove the pins. Press well.

2 Glue the two stiff card base pieces together for a firmer construction. Kraft paper flaps onto the base as described on page 17.

3 Paste glue in a 1.5 cm (⅝ in) border at the bottom of one of the sides. Position against the base at an angle, then glue the second (adjoining) side in the same way and position against the base and the first side, so that the sides meet and abut. Kraft the angle on the inside and the outside.

Continue with side three and finally side four. Check that all angles inside and out have been krafted.

4 Paste glue over one side of the bin and place a piece of outer fabric centrally over this. Trim the excess fabric to 1 cm (⅜ in) on the sides and base and 2 cm (¾ in) on the shaped edge. Trim the excess fabric at the corners.

Paste a thin border of glue on the base, fold over the fabric and stick down. Clip "V" shapes in the fabric overlap on the top shaped edge and glue down, then fold and glue down the two side flaps. Repeat to cover the opposite side.

5 Paste glue over the third side and apply the outer fabric centrally. Trim the excess fabric to 1 cm (⅜ in) on the base and 2 cm (¾ in) on the top shaped edge. Trim the excess fabric at the corners.

Cut the fabric at the sides so that it lies flush along the length of the corner edges. As you are not cutting along the grain of the fabric, it is a little more difficult to do this neatly. However, you can trim off any long threads, paste a very little glue along the edge, then, with a cotton cloth, gently wipe away the excess glue. This will help both to bind the loose threads together and to prevent further fraying.

Clip "V" shapes in the fabric overlap on the top shaped edge and glue this and the base flaps down. Repeat for the remaining side. Trim the piece of lining fabric to fit the outer base and glue in place.

6 Trim the sides and base of each thin card side piece until the card fits neatly but loosely in place sitting approximately 2 mm (1/12 in) below the rim of the bin. Cover with lining fabric, then, following the sequence for lining with cards described on page 24, glue in the sides.

Trim the inner thin card base to fit, cover and glue in position.

TOOLS

1 cm (⅜ in) flat glue brush
2 cm (¾ in) flat glue brush
glue
point turner
scissors
cutting mat
steel ruler
set square
craft knife
pencil

MATERIALS

stiff card: 64 x 95 cm
  (25 x 38 in)
thin card: 64 x 95 cm
  (25 x 38 in)
outer fabric: 68 x 74 cm
  (27 x 29 in)
lining fabric: 72 x 97 cm
  (29 x 39 in)
kraft paper strips

Pieces required
stiff card
sides: 32 x 35 cm
  (12½ x 13¾ in) – cut four
base: 24.6 x 25 cm
  (9⁵⁄₆ x 10) – cut two

thin card
sides: 32 x 35 cm
  (12½ x 13¾ in) – cut four
base: 24.6 x 25 cm
  (9⁵⁄₆ x 10) – cut one

outer fabric
sides: 34 x 37 cm
  (13⅓ x 14½ in) – cut four

lining fabric
sides: 36 x 36 cm
  (14¼ x 14¼ in) – cut four
base: 25 x 25 cm
  (10 x 10 in) – cut two

PREPARATION

Using the template given on the folded sheet at the back of the book, cut out in stiff and thin card and label the four sides of the bin. Cut out and label two bases in stiff card and one in thin.

Cut out and label the outer and lining fabric following the cutting plans on page 110.

STORAGE BIN

Stiff card

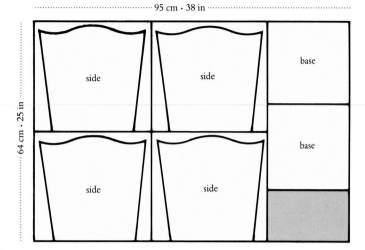

Thin card

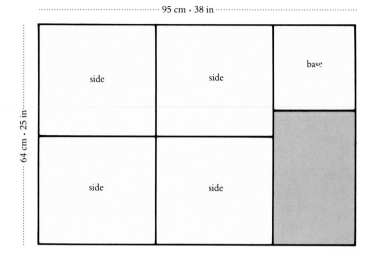

Outer fabric

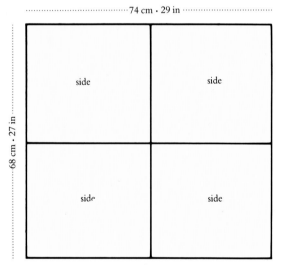

Lining fabric

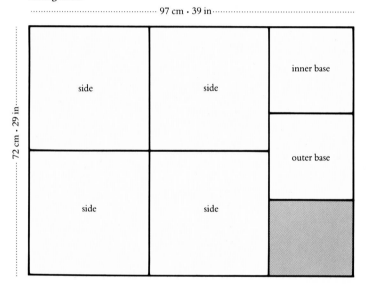

BATHROOM TRAY

Lining fabric

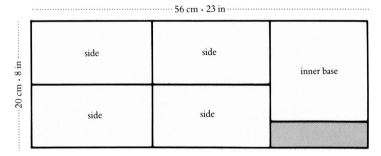

Stiff and thin card

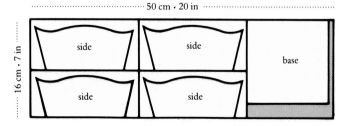

The template for this tray is included on the folded sheet inside the back cover and the method of making is exactly the same as for the bin.

We appliquéd the smallest bird to the inside base, then covered the lining cards with fabric both for increased stability and a neater appearance.

111

Bathroom Tray

TOOLS

1 cm (⅜ in) flat glue brush
2 cm (¾ in) flat glue brush
glue
point turner
scissors
cutting mat
steel ruler
set square
craft knife
pencil
eyelet makers and eyelets

MATERIALS

stiff card: 16 x 50 cm
  (7 x 20 in)
thin card: 16 x 50 cm
  (7 x 20 in)
outer fabric: 32 x 32 cm
  (13 x 13 in)
lining fabric: 20 x 56 cm
  (8 x 23 in)
kraft paper strips

Pieces required
stiff and thin card
sides: 8 x 18 cm (3⅛ x 7 in)
  – cut four
base: 13.3 x 13.7 cm
  (5¼ x 5⅓ in) – cut one

lining fabric
sides: 10 x 20 cm (4 x 8 in)
  – cut four
base: 16 x 16 cm
  (6¼ x 6¼ in) – cut one

PREPARATION

Cut out and label the four
sides of the tray in stiff and
thin card using the template
given on the folded sheet at
the back of the book.
Cut out and label base pieces
each measuring 13.3 x 13.7
cm (5¼ x 5⅓ in), one in stiff
card and one in thin.
  Cut out and label the
lining fabric following the
cutting plan on page 110.

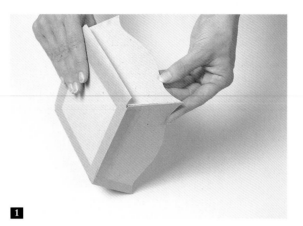

1

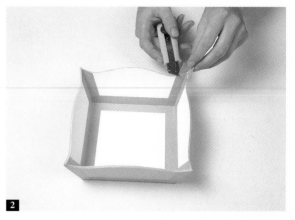

2

3

MAKING UP

1 If using an applied motif, cut it out and
pin it at 1 cm (⅜ in) intervals centrally to
the lining fabric for the inside base of the tray.
Machine in position using a satin stitch or
hand sew with a blanket stitch. Remove the
pins. Press well.

2 Kraft paper flaps onto the base as
described on page 17. Glue one of the
sides at an angle to the base, then the second
(adjoining) side, so that the sides meet and
abut. Kraft the angle, inside and out.
Continue with side three, carefully lining this
up with the previous side (**1**) and finally side
four. Check that all angles inside and out are
krafted. Trim the excess kraft paper to the
shape of the tray (**2**).

3 Paste glue over the base of the tray and
place centrally on the reverse of the outer
fabric. Glue two opposite sides and pull the
fabric up against the sides; press firmly.

4 Cut the fabric at the corners, so that there
is a 1 cm (⅜ in) overlap at each corner
which folds onto the adjoining side (**3**). Stick
these flaps down and trim the excess fabric on
the top to 2 cm (¾ in), following the shape of
the curve. Clip along the length of the curve
to within 3 mm (⅛ in) of the card. Trim away
the excess fabric at the corners and glue the
fabric down to the inside of the tray sides.

5 On a flat surface, tip the box onto one of
its uncovered sides with the fabric underneath. With a pencil, lightly mark the length
of both corners on the reverse of the fabric.
Cut along these lines in order to trim the
fabric to the exact size of the side. Glue in
place, trim the top edge to 2 cm (¾ in), clip
and glue down to the inside. Repeat for the
remaining side.

6 Trim all three straight edges on each side
of the lining cards until they fit their
respective sides neatly but loosely inside the
tray when placed 2 mm (¹⁄₁₂ in) below the top
edge of the tray.

7 Cover with lining fabric, then, following
the sequence for lining with cards
described on page 24, glue in the sides.
  Trim the inner thin card base to fit, cover
and glue in position.

Bathroom boxes

We chose the smaller ducks from the printed fabric design and cut them out with a 5 mm (¼ in) tolerance all round to prevent fraying and to keep the whole duck visible within the satin-stitched edge. To appliqué the ducks to the box fabric, cut out the side pieces and position centrally. Pin at 1 cm (⅜ in) intervals and stitch in place. Blanket stitch by hand or machine a light satin stitch.

The ducks are most effective on the sides of the larger boxes but may be used on the lid of the smallest box.

Follow the method shown on pages 17 and 22 for a box with a separate lid. We give three cutting plans on the following pages but you may adapt to any other size, using the formulae given on page 16 and increasing the weight of the card as the box becomes larger. The boxes are all lined with fabric-covered card.

1 *Small box*

MATERIALS

stiff card: 36 x 30 cm
  (15 x 12 in)
thin card: 48 x 25 cm
  (19 x 10 in)
outer fabric: 50 x 43 cm
  (20 x 17 in)
lining fabric: 28 x 56 cm
  (12 x 23 in)

Pieces required
stiff card

box adjacent: 12 x 12 cm
  ($4\frac{3}{4}$ x $4\frac{3}{4}$ in) – cut two
box upper: 11.6 x 11.8 cm
  ($4\frac{7}{12}$ x $4\frac{2}{3}$ in) – cut two
box base: 11.6 x 12 cm
  ($4\frac{7}{12}$ x $4\frac{3}{4}$ in) – cut one
lid: 12.3 x 12.7 cm
  ($4\frac{5}{6}$ x 5 in) – cut one
lid adjacent: 12.7 x 2.7 cm
  (5 x $1\frac{1}{2}$ in) – cut two
lid upper: 12.3 x 2.5 cm
  ($4\frac{5}{6}$ x 1 in) – cut two

thin card

lid: 12.3 x 12.3 cm
  ($4\frac{5}{6}$ x $4\frac{5}{6}$ in) – cut one
outer base: 11.8 x 11.8 cm
  ($4\frac{2}{3}$ x $4\frac{2}{3}$ in) – cut one
sides and inner base:
11.6 x 11.6 cm ($4\frac{7}{12}$ x $4\frac{7}{12}$)
  – cut five

outer fabric

sides: 50 x 16 cm
  ($19\frac{3}{4}$ x $6\frac{1}{4}$ in) – cut one
lid: 27 x 27 cm (11 x 11 in)
  – cut one

lining fabric

As thin card but adding 2 cm
($\frac{3}{4}$ in) to each measurement

2 *Medium box*

stiff card: 42 x 39 cm
  (17 x 16 in)
thin card: 32 x 54 cm
  (13 x 21 in)
outer fabric: 49 x 66 cm
  (20 x 26 in)
lining fabric: 36 x 62 cm
  (15 x 25 in)

Pieces required
stiff card

box adjacent: 13 x 16 cm
  ($5\frac{1}{12}$ x $6\frac{1}{3}$ in) – cut two
box upper: 12.8 x 15.6 cm
  (5 x $6\frac{1}{6}$ in) – cut two
box base: 15.6 x 16 cm
  ($6\frac{1}{6}$ x $6\frac{1}{3}$ in) – cut one
lid: 16.3 x 16.7 cm

BATHROOM BOXES

Stiff card (small)

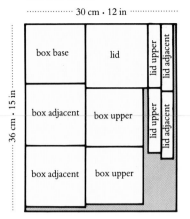

Thin card (small)

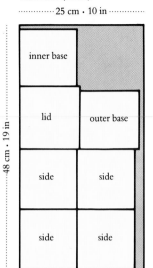

Outer fabric (small)

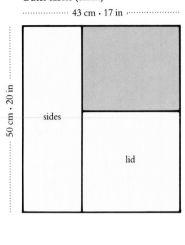

Stiff card (medium)

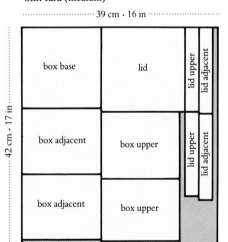

Outer fabric (medium)

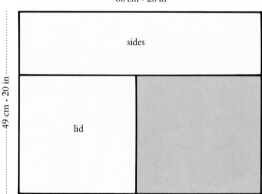

Thin card (medium)

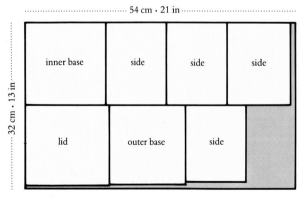

Stiff card (large)

49 cm · 20 in
50 cm · 20 in

box base | lid | lid adjacent | lid upper
box adjacent | box upper
box adjacent | box upper | lid adjacent | lid upper

Thin card (large)

41 cm · 17 in
63 cm · 25 in

side | side
side | outer base
side
side
inner base | lid

Outer fabric (large)

59 cm · 24 in
85 cm · 34 in

sides
lid

Outer fabric – matching fabric for all 3 boxes

76 cm · 31 in
116 cm · 46 in

sides (small) | lid (small)
sides (large) | lid (medium)
sides (medium) | lid (large)

($6 \frac{5}{12}$ x $6 \frac{1}{2}$ in) – cut one
lid adjacent: 16.7 x 3.2 cm
($6 \frac{1}{2}$ x 1 $\frac{1}{4}$ in) – cut two
lid upper: 16.3 x 3 cm
($6 \frac{5}{12}$ x $1 \frac{1}{6}$ in) – cut two

thin card
lid: 16.3 x 16.3 cm
($6 \frac{5}{12}$ x $6 \frac{5}{12}$ in) – cut one
outer base: 15.8 x 15.8 cm
($6 \frac{1}{4}$ x $6 \frac{1}{4}$ in) – cut one
inner base: 15.6 x 15.6 cm
($6 \frac{1}{6}$ x $6 \frac{1}{6}$ in) – cut one
sides: 15.6 x 12.6 cm
($6 \frac{1}{6}$ x $4 \frac{11}{12}$ in) – cut four

outer fabric
sides: 17 x 66 cm (7 x 26 in)
– cut one
lid: 32 x 32 cm (13 x 13 in)
– cut one

lining fabric (see small box)

3 Large box

stiff card: 50 x 49 cm
(20 x 20 in)
thin card: 63 x 41 cm
(25 x 17 in)
outer fabric: 85 x 59 cm
(34 x 24 in)
lining fabric: 45 x 71 cm
(18 x 29 in)

Pieces required
stiff card
box adjacent: 14.5 x 20.5 cm
($5 \frac{3}{4}$ x $8 \frac{1}{2}$ in) – cut two
box upper: 14.3 x 20.1 cm
($5 \frac{2}{3}$ x $7 \frac{11}{12}$ in) – cut two
box base: 20.1 x 20.5 cm
($7 \frac{11}{12}$ x $8 \frac{1}{2}$ in) – cut one
lid: 20.8 x 21.2 cm
($8 \frac{1}{4}$ x $8 \frac{5}{12}$ in) – cut one
lid adjacent: 21.2 x 3.7 cm
($8 \frac{5}{12}$ x $1 \frac{5}{12}$ in) – cut two
lid upper: 20.8 x 3.5 cm
($8 \frac{1}{4}$ x $1 \frac{1}{3}$ in) – cut two

thin card
lid: 20.8 x 20.8 cm
($8 \frac{1}{4}$ x $8 \frac{1}{4}$ in) – cut one
outer base: 20.3 x 20.3 cm
(8 x 8 in) – cut one
inner base: 20.1 x 20.1 cm
($7 \frac{11}{12}$ x $7 \frac{11}{12}$ in) – cut one
sides: 14.1 x 20.1 cm
($5 \frac{1}{2}$ x $7 \frac{11}{12}$ in) – cut four

outer fabric
sides: 85 x 18.5 cm
($33 \frac{1}{2}$ x $7 \frac{1}{2}$ in) – cut one
lid: 40 x 40 cm (16 x 16 in)
– cut one

lining fabric (see small box)

The
MUSIC ROOM

Although the items shown here have been specifically designed to keep sheet music, music books and papers tidy and filed in order, you do not have to be a musician to find a use for any of these folders. We simply chose a fabric to suit the subject which we wanted to organize.

Your hobbies may include music but are likely to be several and diverse. If you like to cook and to garden you will almost certainly have piles of catalogues, leaflets or magazine cuttings which you have kept for reference. Choose a fabric with a specific design to help you to identify the folders immediately.

The papers folders are so easy to make that you can produce one for each new project - building a home extension, arranging a holiday, organizing the village fête, making costumes for the school play - they have limitless potential and possibilities.

The waste bin, of course, can be made for any room and covered in any fabric which will not show dirt easily and which will work with your room scheme.

Portfolio

TOOLS

1 cm (⅜ in) flat glue brush
2 cm (¾ in) flat glue brush
glue
point turner
scissors
cutting mat
steel ruler
set square
craft knife
pencil

MATERIALS

stiff card: 47 x 140 cm
  (19 x 55 in) or 47 x 70 cm
  (19 x 27½ in) if using
  4 mm/⅙ in thick card
  - see below)
thin card: 42 x 107 cm
  (17 x 42 in)
outer fabric: 51 x 74 cm
  (20 x 29 in)
contrast fabric: 51 x 77 cm
  (20 x 31 in)
lining or paper-backed fabric:
  57 x 58 cm (23 x 23 in)
fastening: cord and tassel
  (optional)

Pieces required
stiff card
front and backs: 47 x 35 cm
  (18½ x 13¾ in)
  - cut four (see below)

thin card
insides: 34.5 x 46.5 cm
  (13½ x 18¼ in) - cut two
vertical pocket:
  7.5 x 46.5 cm (3 x 18¼ in)
  - cut one
horizontal pocket:
  34.5 x 12 cm (13½ x 4 in)
  - cut one
pad holder:
  34.5 x 2 cm (13½ x ¾ in)
  - cut one
inner corners: 7 x 7 cm
  (3 x 3 in) - cut one

Note, the portfolio can be
made with just two
rectangles of stiff card but
will be more robust if you
cut four and glue together in
pairs. Alternatively, of
course, you could cut two
rectangles of thicker card.

Continued on page 120

MAKING UP

1 Paste glue to one of the pieces of stiff card. Place one of the outer fabric pieces right side down on the work surface. Position the card on the fabric, so that one long side of the card is flush with one long side of the fabric, leaving an equal overlap on the remaining three sides. Turn the card over and press firmly with the palms of your hands. Clip the fabric across the two outside corners to within 5 mm (¼ in) of the card (or to within 7 mm/5⁄16 in if using very thick card).

Glue down all three flaps onto the stiff card, using a point turner to neaten the corners. Leave under weights and repeat with the other outside card.

Note: If your fabric has a definite pattern, make sure you have a front and a back. The raw edge of the fabric covering the card will be on the spine side of the finished folder.

2 Cover one of the pieces of thin card with glue and centre this on the wrong side of one of the pieces of lining or paper-backed fabric, leaving an equal overlap on all sides. Cut across each corner to within 2 mm (1⁄12 in) of the card and glue all overlaps down. Repeat for the other inner card. Place under weights.

3 To make the outer corners, cut the relevant piece of lining or paper-backed fabric diagonally into four triangles. Place one of the corner pieces face down on the work surface. Position one of the outside portfolio corners (i.e. not the raw edge side) over this piece, leaving a 1.5 cm (⅝ in) overlap on both sides. Pencil round the corner, thus marking the exact area to be glued.

Carefully paste glue within the pencilled area, reposition the right side of the portfolio on top. Press into place. Turn back and cut across the excess fabric at the corner to within 5 mm (¼ in) of the card. Glue the corner flaps, fold over each one in turn and press firmly, using the point turner to neaten. Repeat for the other three outside corners.

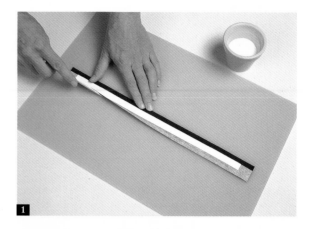

4 To make the pad holder, glue the strip of card and place centrally on the reverse of the lining fabric, fold over the top and bottom with the point turner and glue down (1). Place right side down on the work surface. Take one of the covered inner cards, mark on the back where you wish the pad holder to be, then place, right side down, onto the pad holder and glue the two side flaps in place.

5 To make the horizontal pocket, glue the relevant piece of card and place centrally on the fabric. Fold over one long side and glue down. This will be the top of the pocket. Trim across the bottom corners to within 5 mm (¼ in) of the card. Place the pocket right side down. Lay the side you are working on, right side down, so that the bottom lines up exactly with the card on the pocket, leaving three flaps showing. Fold these over and glue round the bottom of the inner card (2).

Useful for carrying music books and score sheets, the expanding spine also allows many sheets to be kept flat for storage. I use one of these portfolios for each design scheme which I am working on, keeping everything in it from the original sketches to the finished plans, drawings and fabric samples, then I use it to set off the designs when I finally present the scheme to my client. Once the job is finished, these portfolios also make excellent files for storing all the large papers and drawings.

The basic method given is flexible, so that you can choose any combination of vertical and horizontal pockets, corner pockets, bars and ties and adjust our measurements to produce any size of portfolio to suit your own special requirements, matching the outer fabric to the contents.

Continued from page 118

outer fabric
outsides: 51 x 37 cm
  (20 x 14½ in) – cut two

contrast fabric
sides: 50.5 x 38.5 cm
  (19¾ x 15¼ in) – cut two

lining or paper-backed fabric
vertical pocket:
  50.5 x 11.5 cm
  (20 x 4½ in) – cut one
outer spine:
  51 x 14 cm (20 x 5½ in)
  – cut one
inner spine: 46.5 x 12 cm
  (18¼ x 4¾ in) – cut one
pad holder:
  38.5 x 4 cm (15 x 1½ in)
  – cut one
horizontal pocket:
  38.5 x 16 cm (15 x 6¼ in)
  – cut one
inner corners: 12 x 12 cm
  (5 x 5 in) – cut one
outer corners: 13 x 6.5 cm
  (5 x 2½ in) – cut one

PREPARATION

Cut out and label all the pieces in the two cards and the three fabrics following the cutting plans on page 121.

Glue the two stiff card rectangles together if using 2 mm (1/12 in) card.

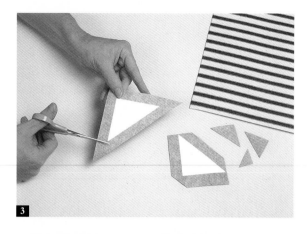

3

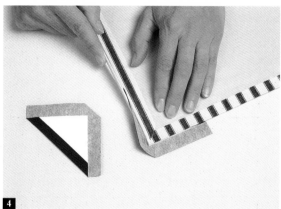

4

6 To make the vertical pocket, work exactly as for the horizontal pocket but line up on the long side of the second inner card.

7 To make the inner corners, take the 7 cm (3 in) square piece of thin card and cut into two triangles. Cut the 12 cm (5 in) square piece of lining fabric into two triangles. Place the card centrally on the reverse of the fabric and trim off the excess fabric at the corners (3). Fold over and glue the long side.

8 Position the corners on the inner card so that the right side of the card is against the wrong side of the corner piece. Working from the wrong side, fold over the remaining two sides and glue down (4).

9 To make the spine, place the outer spine face down and mark two lines down the length, 3.5 cm (1⅓ in) in from each side, and one line across the width, 2 cm (¾ in) down from the top. Paste glue onto one of the 3.5 cm (1⅓ in) strips below the 2 cm (¾ in) line. Take one of the outside portfolio pieces

and position this onto the spine, right side down, lining up the pencil line with the raw fabric edge, with equal overlap at top and bottom. Turn over and press firmly. Repeat this for the other side, checking that the front and back covers are exactly aligned at the top and bottom. Spread glue onto the top and bottom flaps and stick down.

10 Glue the inner spine in place, so that it covers the gap between the two portfolio sides (5). Keep flat until dry.

11 If required, glue a loop of cord in the middle of one of the outer folio edges. Glue the tassel to the opposite edge.

12 Spread glue evenly all over the reverse of one of the inner pieces, then press firmly into position on one of the portfolio sides. Repeat with the other side and leave under weights until dry. When completely dry, fold the portfolio in half, line up the front and back covers, then push the spine in along its length (6).

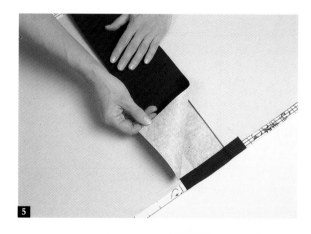

5

6

PORTFOLIO

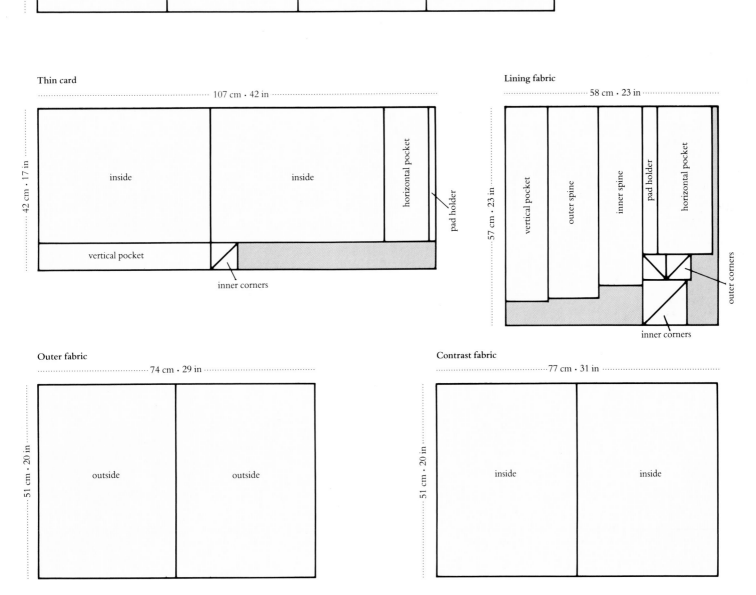

Stiff card

140 cm · 55 in

47 cm · 19 in

| front | front | back | back |

Thin card

107 cm · 42 in

42 cm · 17 in

inside | inside | horizontal pocket | pad holder

vertical pocket

inner corners

Lining fabric

58 cm · 23 in

57 cm · 23 in

vertical pocket | outer spine | inner spine | pad holder | horizontal pocket

outer corners

inner corners

Outer fabric

74 cm · 29 in

51 cm · 20 in

outside | outside

Contrast fabric

77 cm · 31 in

51 cm · 20 in

inside | inside

Papers Folder

TOOLS

1 cm (⅜ in) flat glue brush
2 cm (¾ in) flat glue brush
glue
point turner
scissors
cutting mat
steel ruler
set square
craft knife
pencil

MATERIALS

stiff card: 35 x 50 cm
 (14 x 20 in)
thin card: 34 x 48 cm
 (14 x 19 in)
outer fabric: 38 x 56 cm
 (15 x 22 in)
lining fabric: 37 x 54 cm
 (15 x 21 in)
ribbon: 2.2 m (2¼ yds) long,
 15 mm (½ in) wide

Pieces required

stiff card: 35 x 25 cm
 (14 x 10 in) – cut two
thin card: 34 x 24 cm
 (13½ x 9½ in) – cut two
outer fabric: 38 x 28 cm
 (15 x 11 in) – cut two
lining fabric: 37 x 27 cm
 (14½ x 10½ in) – cut two

PREPARATION

Cut all the pieces of card and
fabric in half following the
measurements given above
and trimming to size where
necessary.

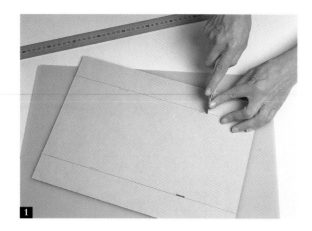

MAKING UP

1 To make the ribbon holes, take one of
the pieces of stiff card and mark a pencil
line 4.5 cm (1¾ in) in from each long side
down the length of the card. From one short
edge, measure 9 cm (3½ in) down this line
and mark, then a further 1.5 cm (⅝ in) and
mark. Pencil over this 1.5 cm (⅝ in) section
more heavily, then draw another line 1.5 cm
(⅝ in) long parallel to this but 3 mm (⅛ in)
towards the inside of the card. Join the lines
to make a narrow rectangle, then cut this out
with craft knife and ruler.

Repeat, this time measuring in from the
opposite short edge but along the same
pencilled line, then make two more holes in
corresponding positions along the second
pencilled line **(1)**. Repeat the whole process
on the other piece of stiff card.

Cut ribbon holes in the thin card in the
same way but make the pencil lines 4 cm
(1½ in) in from each side and mark 8.5 cm
(3⅜ in) down the line, then another 1.5 cm
(⅝ in). Before going any further, it's a good
idea to line up the pieces of stiff card with
their corresponding pieces of thin card to
check that the alignment of the ribbon holes is
exact. Adjust if necessary.

2 Paste glue to the outside of one piece of
stiff card and cover with one piece of the
outer fabric, making sure that any pattern is
centred. Smooth away any bubbles. Trim the
excess fabric to 1.5 cm (⅝ in) all round. Trim
across each corner to within 5 mm (¼ in) of
the card, fold over the edges and glue down.
From the back of the card, cut into the middle
of the ribbon holes. Paste glue round the hole
on the back of the card and use the point
turner to push the fabric sections through
from the front to neaten the opening **(2)**.

Repeat with the other side and with the
lining cards.

3 Glue the reverse of the lining cards. Place
the covered lining cards centrally on the
reverse of the outer cards, lining up the ribbon
holes. Place under weights and leave to dry.

When completely dry, cut the ribbon into
two equal pieces, thread through the holes to
make an expanding file, tie into bows and
neaten the ends.

I first saw folders similar to this one in a museum exhibition. They held personal letters which the owner had filed neatly by year and by writer. These folders were well over a hundred years old and the outsides were covered not in fabric but with hand-made, marbled papers.

Our fabric-covered folder will take you under half an hour to make from start to finish - so in one weekend you could make enough folders to sort out all your loose papers.

Use denim with string to tie, gingham with webbing tape for more informal use, or an elegant stripe or a pretty chintz with satin ribbon.

Alternatively, choose your outer covers in paper or fabrics to suit the subject - a fabric with a herb motif for your cookery files, topiary trees for garden information, small birds to hold the records of a bird-watching hobby - see page 78 for some of the many possibilities.

This music holder is, in fact, just a simple version of the portfolio without pockets and corners but with a contrasting border on the front edge and a tasselled closure. If ribbons were used instead to secure the music sheets during transport, they could also be used to mark the page when you are practising.

124

Music Holder

MAKING UP

1 Place the main fabric, right side down, on the work surface. Arrange the stiff card pieces with the long, narrow piece of thin card between them, so that there is an equal overlap of fabric at the top and bottom and so that the outer side edges of the stiff card are parallel to the raw edges of the fabric. Glue in place. Fold over the excess fabric at top and bottom and glue.

2 Take the inner spine piece of paper-backed fabric and glue this over the piece of thin card. Next take the other two strips of paper-backed fabric and mark a pencil line centrally along the length of each strip. Paste glue very carefully along the length of one half of the pencil line and stick in place on the front of the folder, so that the pencil mark lines up with the edge of the folder and there

is an equal overlap at top and bottom. Trim away the excess fabric at the corners, fold the top flap down and the bottom flap up, glue in place, then fold in the entire length of the side edging and glue into place. Repeat for the other side.

3 Glue a loop of cord in the middle of the inside of the outside back of the holder. Glue the tassel in the corresponding position on the opposite edge.

4 Take the two side pieces of thin card and cover with fabric. Glue the left hand side in place, lining the right hand edge of this piece of card with the right hand edge of the stiff card. This will mean that a larger strip of the edging will be seen when the folder is open. Glue the right hand side in the same way. Place under weights and leave until completely dry.

TOOLS

1 cm (⅜ in) flat glue brush
2 cm (¾ in) flat glue brush
glue
point turner
scissors
cutting mat
steel ruler
set square
craft knife
pencil

MATERIALS

stiff card: 42 x 58 cm
 (17 x 23 in)
thin card: 42 x 57 cm
 (17 x 23 in)
main fabric: 47 x 121 cm
 (18 x 48 in)
paper-backed fabric:
 46 x 18 cm (18 x 8 in)
cord and tassel for fastening

Pieces required
stiff card
sides: 41.5 x 29 cm
 (16½ x 11½ in) – cut two

thin card
sides: 41 x 27.5 cm
 (16⅛ x 10⅞ in) – cut two
spine strengthener:
 41.5 x 2 cm (16½ x ¾ in)
 – cut one

main fabric
backs: 46.5 x 60 cm
 (18 x 23¾ in) – cut one
insides: 44 x 30.5 cm
 (17½ x 12 in) – cut two

paper-backed fabric
outer edges: 45.5 x 6 cm
 (18 x 2½ in) – cut two
inner spine: 41 x 6 cm
 (16⅛ x 2½ in) – cut one

PREPARATION

Cut out and label all the pieces in stiff and thin card, main and paper-backed fabric following the cutting plans opposite.

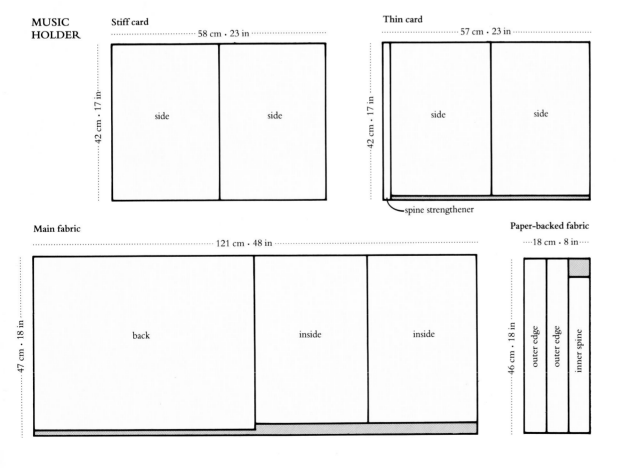

MUSIC HOLDER

Stiff card
58 cm · 23 in
42 cm · 17 in
side   side

Thin card
57 cm · 23 in
42 cm · 17 in
side   side
spine strengthener

Main fabric
121 cm · 48 in
47 cm · 18 in
back   inside   inside

Paper-backed fabric
18 cm · 8 in
46 cm · 18 in
outer edge   outer edge   inner spine

Waste Bin

MATERIALS

stiff card: 46 x 110 cm
  (19 x 44 in)
outer fabric: 50 x 130 cm
  (20 x 52 in)
paper-backed fabric:
  46 x 110 cm (19 x 44 in)
kraft paper strips

Pieces required
stiff card
sides: 4 pieces as per template
base: 18.6 x 19 cm
  (7⅓ x 7½ in) - cut two

outer fabric
sides: 4 pieces as per template
  plus a 2 cm (¾ in) turning
  allowance all round

paper-backed fabric
sides: 4 pieces as per template
base: 18.6 x 19 cm
  (7⅓ x 7½ in) - cut two

PREPARATION

Construct a template from
the dimensions given in the
diagram below. Cut out and
label all the pieces in stiff
card, outer and paper-backed
fabric following the cutting
plan below but adding a
turning allowance of 2 cm
(¾ in) all round each piece
for the outer fabric. Use a
ruler and pencil to draw the
shapes on the fabric.

MAKING UP

Follow the instructions for
the storage bin on page 109
but note that this bin is lined
with paper-backed fabric
only.

**We designed this bin
specifically to fit this
fabric but it is a useful size
and a fun shape to work
with. If you prefer a less
sharp point, keep the
vertical centre height,
width and base measure-
ments but lengthen the
side to 30 cm (12 in).**

Stiff card

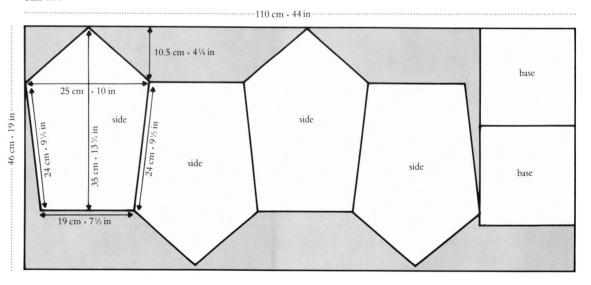

110 cm · 44 in

10.5 cm · 4⅛ in

25 cm · 10 in

46 cm · 19 in

24 cm · 9½ in

35 cm · 13¾ in

side

24 cm · 9½ in

side

side

side

side

base

base

19 cm · 7½ in

INDEX

SUPPLIES AND KITS

All of the projects shown in this book are available in kit form
from The Cartonnage Co. We can supply all tools necessary for cartonnage,
including paper-backed fabric in a variety of colours. Free help and advice is available
during normal working hours. The Cartonnage Co. runs workshops
based on a one or two day course, please ask for details.

If you would like a brochure and price list or any information
about cartonnage please contact:

The Cartonnage Co.
Hill House
Creech St Michael
Taunton
Somerset TA3 5DP

Telephone: 01823 443335
Fax: 01823 442711